KIDS' BIG QUESTIONS FOR GOD

Other Books by Sandy Silverthorne

KIDS' BIG QUESTIONS FOR GOD

101 Things You Want to Know

SANDY SILVERTHORNE

Revell

a division of Baker Publishing Group
Grand Rapids, Michigan

© 2023 by Sandy Silverthorne

Published by Revell
a division of Baker Publishing Group
PO Box 6287, Grand Rapids, MI 49516-6287
www.revellbooks.com

Printed in the United States of America

Library of Congress Cataloging-in-Publication Data
Names: Silverthorne, Sandy, 1951- author.
Title: Kids' big questions for God : 101 things you want to know / Sandy
    Silverthorne.
Description: Grand Rapids : Revell, a division of Baker Publishing Group, 2023.
    | Audience: Ages 6-10 | Audience: Grades 2-3
Identifiers: LCCN 2022028666 | ISBN 9780800741761 (paperback) | ISBN
    9781493439874 (ebook)
Subjects: LCSH: God (Christianity)—Juvenile literature. | God
    (Christianity)—Miscellanea.
Classification: LCC BT107 .S55 2023 | DDC 231—dc23/eng/20220803
LC record available at https://lccn.loc.gov/2022028666

The author is represented by WordServe Literary Group, www.wordserveliterary.com.

Baker Publishing Group publications use paper produced from sustainable forestry practices and post-consumer waste whenever possible.

23   24   25   26   27   28   29   7   6   5   4   3   2   1

To Vicki:
It's such an adventure discovering
the big questions in life with you.

To Christy:
I am so proud of who you're becoming in the Lord.
Plus, we do have a lot of fun together.

To the kids and leaders at Camp Harlow in Oregon:
You were the first ones to inspire this book with your
amazing, big questions. Love being with you guys.

CONTENTS

Contents

Contents

Contents

Contents

Contents

Contents

Introduction

Got questions?

Who created God? How old is He? Will there be animals in heaven? Why did God create mosquitoes? These and tons of other questions kids wonder about are all answered in this fun, informative book. Did Jesus really walk on water? Did He really heal people? Why? Where does God live? Why does bad stuff happen? Sometimes when we're getting to know God, we might think it's not okay to ask questions. After all, aren't we just supposed to trust Him and do what He says? Absolutely. God knows what's best for us, so we can always trust Him. But it's also okay to wonder about things. In fact, He wants us to come to Him for answers to all of life's questions—BIG and small.

Hopefully this book will help answer a lot of your questions about God, but always remember, there are some things about Him we'll never be able to figure out. After all, He's so GINORMOUS and SUPER SMART that some things we'll just have to trust Him with. Meanwhile, let's get started. Let's search for the answers to some BIG questions for God.

One way to use this book is to read one of these questions a day as a devotion in the morning or evening. Or feel free to read as many as you want at one time. It's up to you!

By the way, as you go through this book, you'll discover some Bible verses. They'll look like this: Genesis 1:3–5 or John 3:16. If you have a Bible with you, try looking up the verses we talk about. Your mom or dad might help you with this. That way you'll discover some new things and start to learn how to study your Bible.

Who created God?

You have always been, and you will always be.

Psalm 90:2

Since everything we know in our lives had a beginning, this is a perfectly natural question to ask. After all, your cat or dog was born at some point. Somebody built the house you live in, and even your school was constructed once. Those big trees outside started as tiny little seeds, and come to think of it, even you were born! So, who created God? Well, get ready to have your brain expanded.

You ready? Here it comes . . . Nobody created God! And to make things even harder to understand . . . get ready . . . He's been around forever! He never began. He's always been here. Whoa. I need to sit down for a second. Yup, the Bible (we'll talk more about that soon) says that God has been around forever. Check out what Psalm 90:2 says about God: "Before the mountains were born, and before you created the earth and the world, you are God. You have always been, and you will always be."

Whoa. And get ready for this: Not only has God been around forever, but He's going to *be* around forever too. Wow, that's a long time and that's some big God we're talking about. So, the answer to the question "Who created God?" is nobody! He's the beginning of life itself!

How old is God?

To you, a thousand years
  is like the passing of a day.
  It passes like an hour in the night.

Psalm 90:4

This kind of goes along with the last question, "Who created God?" Since God was never created and He has no beginning, there's no way to say how old He is. You see, here's another one of those explode-your-brain facts about God. Okay, you ready? He lives outside of time.

In fact, God *created* time. Whoa! What's that again? Yeah, I know. Let me say it again. God created time. Look at Genesis 1:3–5 (the first book in the Bible): "Then God said, 'Let there be light.' And light appeared. And God was pleased with it and divided the light from the darkness. He called the light 'daytime,' and the darkness 'nighttime.' Together they formed the first day" (TLB). Then verses 16–19 say that God made the sun and the moon and basically created a day—time—and there we

explode-your-brain facts

have it! In fact, if you really want to check it out, look at Psalm 118:24: "This is the day the Lord has made. We will rejoice and be glad in it" (TLB).

See, God actually made days! Hard to understand, isn't it? It's easier to wrap your head around the fact that He created the mountains and the oceans and the rivers and you and me, but creating time? How does somebody do that? Good question. I don't know, but He did. So you see, God's not limited by time because He's outside of it and even created it. That's how He can always be around forever.

Happy Birthday, GOD!

Above and Beyond

Impress your parents! Tell them that God is a *transcendent* God. That means He's above and beyond everything: space, time, the world, the universe—everything. Explain this to your parents; they'll be really impressed.

Why did God create the world? Was He lonely?

> So God created human beings in his image. In the image of God he created them. He created them male and female.
>
> Genesis 1:27

That's a great question, and no, to start off, God is never lonely. Here's another one of those hard-to-understand facts about God. You know the drill: Hold on to your head. God is one person, but He's also three persons: God the Father, God the Son—Jesus—and God the Holy Spirit. He's three people in one! So be assured, God is never lonely. Then why did He create the world and all the people in it? There are three reasons:

explode-your-brain facts

1. God created us basically to show Himself off! He made people "in His image" so we could reflect what God is like to let everyone know there is a God and that He is love.

2. God made the world because He gets great delight out of creating things. Just look around you. Can you see mountains or rivers? Are there trees? Do you live by, or have you ever visited, the Pacific or Atlantic Ocean? Pretty awesome, isn't it? God is a creative God; it's just who He is. He naturally creates, so He created nature, animals, and you and me!

3. God is filled with love. In fact, He has so much love that He's overflowing with it! He created people in order to share all of His love with us. And guess what? God's still creating things today! Trees, streams, lakes, puppies, kittens, and even new little babies.

Draw a picture of your best friend.

List five things you like about them.

....

....

....

....

....

God Knows Your Name

I've got some questions you can talk over with your mom, dad, or small group. Try reading each question out loud, then let each person answer. Remember, there are no wrong answers; these are here to help you grow in your understanding of who God is.

Did you know that the Bible tells us God is our Father, He knows us by name, and He loves us?

1. God wants to be as close to you as a family member. How does that make you feel?

2. If God were sitting here right now, what would you ask Him?

3. We often think to talk to God about hard stuff we're going through, but did you know that He wants to know all about the good stuff too? What are some good things going on in your life right now?

4. What are some things you might need God's help with right now?

What's the Bible?

Every word of God can be trusted.
He protects those who come to him for safety.

The Bible is a book, or actually a collection of books, written over a period of about 1,500 years. There are sixty-six books altogether, and they were written by about forty writers. The first part of the Bible, the Old Testament, was written in the Hebrew language, while the New Testament, where you'll find the stories about Jesus and His followers, was written in Greek. God used men to write the Bible so we could get to know Him and understand what He's like. While the Bible contains poems, stories, history, and books of wisdom, every single part of the book points us to Jesus. Even the really old stuff in Genesis and Exodus!

Who wrote the Bible?

Write down these words.
Exodus 34:27

The Bible was written by forty different people. Some of them were government officials, like Nehemiah, or God's spokesmen, like Isaiah or Jeremiah. A couple were fishermen: John and Peter. And one was a tax collector: Matthew. King David of Israel (remember David and Goliath?) wrote most of the book of Psalms, and his son Solomon wrote most of the book of Proverbs. Even though the Bible was written over 1,500 years in two different languages, the message is the same: God knows you, He sees you, and He loves you.

In the Beginning

In the Beginning...

Is the Bible for real?

Your word is truth.
John 17:17 ESV

Is the Bible true? Some people doubt that what the Bible says is real, but guess what? No one has ever been able to prove it's not true. In fact, some people have even tried to disprove the stories and ended up believing them and following Jesus. So why should we believe the Bible?

We can believe the Bible for three reasons:

1. *Prophecy.* A long time before Jesus was even born, people received messages from God and wrote them down. These people were called prophets, and their messages all came true. These messages talked about Jesus, God's people, and even world history. Some of these predictions were written hundreds of years before they came true, but they did come true! (See "Some Prophecies about Jesus in the Old Testament" in question 7 for some examples.)

2. *Archaeology.* There are people who study old things and the history of the world. They're called archaeologists, and some of them even get to travel around the world to dig up old bones and buildings and sometimes entire towns! Every year these people discover more and more evidence that the Bible is true and that the people mentioned in it were real people. In just the past couple of decades, archaeologists have discovered the pool where Jesus sent the blind man to wash (see John 9:7), a stone that mentions Governor Pontius Pilate, who handed Jesus over to be crucified (see Mark 15:1–15), and a house that might have belonged to Jesus's good friend Peter.

3. *Jesus.* Jesus trusted in the Scriptures and even quoted them. Of course, they only had what we call the Old Testament at the time Jesus was here on earth, but He trusted God's Word and helped others to trust it too.

If you want to get to know God more, it's a good idea to start reading the Bible. If you don't have one, check with your mom or dad and see if you can get an inexpensive copy at a bookstore or online. But you can also go online and start reading the Bible right now. Just google "Bible." The best place to start reading is in the New Testament.

That's where you'll read all about Jesus. The Bible is God's love letter to you.

Every Day with Jesus

If you want to start reading the Bible and learning more about God and His Son, Jesus, here's a good way to start: Plan to spend five to ten minutes a day reading it, maybe in the morning when you wake up or right before you go to bed at night. A good place to start is the book of Luke in the New Testament. This book tells the stories of Jesus and His friends. Before you start reading, pray that God will show you something in His Word. Then try reading for a few minutes. Pretty soon you'll have read through the whole New Testament! Check out the sample Bible reading plan at the end of this book to give you a start on the book of Luke.

By the way, there are lots of Bibles out there that are written with kids in mind. Some even have pictures and short guides to help you know what's going on in the story. It's important to find a Bible that you like and that you'll want to read every day.

DID YOU KNOW?

According to Genesis 6:15, Noah's ark was at least 450 feet long, 75 feet wide, and 45 feet high. That's about half the size of a modern aircraft carrier. Aircraft carriers are more than 1,000 feet long and can carry over 5,000 people and 90 planes. Some scholars believe the ark could have held as much cargo as 330 railroad cars can!

What's the difference between the Old Testament and the New Testament?

Your word is like a lamp for my feet
and a light for my way.

Psalm 119:105

This is a really good question, especially if you're studying your Bible. The Old Testament came first. It's at the beginning of your Bible. In fact, it starts at the *very* beginning. Genesis 1:1 says, "In the beginning . . ." and we go on to read about how God created the whole world: the sun, the moon, the stars, the animals, and the people. Then we find out how God brought about His special people—the Israelites. The Old Testament tells us about Noah, Moses, Samson, Gideon, David, Solomon, and lots of others. We also meet some prophets who spoke for God, and we meet some kings—some good and some bad.

But, even though Jesus isn't ever mentioned by name in the Old Testament, the whole book is about Him! That's true. Everyone in the Old Testament was waiting for the One who was going to save them and put things right.

In the New Testament, we hear the story of Jesus: His birth, His miracles, His death, the day He rose from the dead, and even when He went up to heaven to live forever. Then, through the rest of the New Testament, we meet a lot of Jesus's early followers either through stories or the letters they wrote. And at the very end of the Bible is the one book that hasn't taken place yet. It's the book about the future—Revelation. The word *revelation* means a vision or message from God. The whole book of Revelation is God's way of saying we win in the end and evil will be defeated.

Old Testament

New Testament

Prophets Moses Kings

Jesus

Some Prophecies about Jesus in the Old Testament

Prophecy	When It Came True
Psalm 8:2: The kids will praise Him.	Matthew 21:15–16
Psalm 41:9: He will be betrayed by a friend.	Luke 22:47
Psalm 22:16: His hands and feet will be pierced.	John 20:27
Psalm 22:18: Soldiers will gamble for His clothes.	Matthew 27:35
Psalm 109:4: He will pray for His enemies.	Luke 23:34
Psalm 16:10: He will rise from the dead!	Matthew 28:7

Who were Adam and Eve?

> So the Lord God caused the man to sleep very deeply. While the man was asleep, God took one of the ribs from the man's body. . . . The Lord God used the rib from the man to make a woman. Then the Lord brought the woman to the man.
>
> Genesis 2:21–22

Adam and Eve were the very first people God created. God made the whole world and the universe. He created all the animals, birds, and fish, then He made Adam, then Eve. They lived in an incredibly beautiful place called the garden of Eden, and they had everything they could possibly want. Plus, they were best friends with God! But God had one rule: Don't eat from the tree of the knowledge of good and evil. But one day, the devil, in the disguise of a snake, tricked Eve and she and Adam both disobeyed God and ate the fruit. After that, their friendship with God was broken. And bad stuff, like sickness, pain, hurt, separation, and death, came into the world. Adam and Eve couldn't live in the garden anymore, and even though God still loved them, things were different.

How did Adam and Eve fill the whole world with people?

God blessed them and said, "Have many children and grow in number. Fill the earth and be its master."

Genesis 1:28

Did you know there are more than seven *billion* people on earth? Wow, that's a lot! So how did all those people come from just two—Adam and Eve? Isn't that impossible? Well, there are a couple things to think about. One is that when Adam and Eve were around, people lived a *lot* longer than they do now. In fact, Adam lived 930 years (Gen. 5:5), and one of his descendants, Methuselah, lived to be 969 years old (Gen. 5:27)! That's a lot of time to have more and more kids. So then, after the big flood during Noah's time, God started over again with just Noah, his wife, his three sons, and their wives.

Noah lived to be 950 years old (Gen. 9:29)! And if they all kept having kids and those kids kept having kids and so forth, after several thousand years, you've got a huge population! It's simple multiplication. Pretty soon people started spreading out all over the region. Some stayed and built the Tower of Babel, and others traveled down as far as Egypt.

Aren't you glad you were born? So is God.

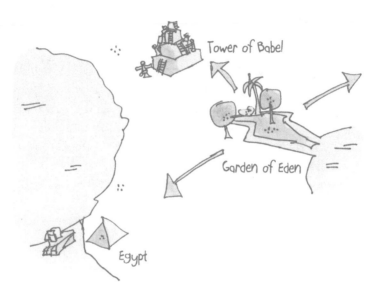

10

Is Jesus really God?

The Father and I are one.
John 10:30

This is really the big question, isn't it? I mean, think about it. Imagine you're hanging out with a guy who's constantly telling you that He's God in human form. That would be pretty confusing, wouldn't it? Especially if He kept doing all these amazing things around you, like healing people, calming storms, and walking on water! So, how do we know if Jesus really was who He said He was?

According to Jesus's own words, as well as the words of the guys who followed Him, the answer to the question of whether Jesus is really God is absolutely YES. God became a man (actually, a little baby just like the rest of us) and, when He was thirty years old, spent about three years in public doing miracles, healing people, and teaching them what God was like. Check out what Jesus said about Himself: "The Father and I are one" (John 10:30) and "Anyone who has seen me has seen the Father!" (John 14:9 TLB).

Since Jesus called Himself equal with God, He leaves us with a few choices: He wasn't God, but He thought He was; He knew He wasn't God, but He told people He was in order to get them to follow Him; or, of course, He was who He said He was, the one and only Son of God. Think about it. Almost all of Jesus's disciples went to their own deaths claiming Jesus was the Son of God. Would someone do that if they knew His story wasn't true? Plus, Jesus did a lot of miracles in front of a lot of people, all of which helped prove He was who He said He was. So Jesus really only leaves us with one choice: number three, He really was God in human form, showing Himself to us. Okay, got it? He was either a liar or our Lord. Pretty simple, don't you think? Jesus was God in the flesh. For real.

11

What's God like?

Part 1

The men were amazed. They said, "What kind of man
is this? Even the wind and the sea obey him!"

Matthew 8:27

One of the reasons Jesus came to earth was to show
us what God the Father was like. Jesus was like
an audiovisual display of who God is. In other words,
whenever we look at Jesus, we know what God is like.
So, what's He like? Well, for one thing, He's pretty
powerful.

One day Jesus and His disciples were out on the Sea
of Galilee when a huge, scary storm came up and almost sank the boat! And what was Jesus doing all this
time? He was sleeping! So they woke Him up, and Jesus
went to the front of the boat and shouted, "Be quiet! Be
still!" to the storm. And it stopped immediately! The
wind died down, the clouds parted, and the sea became
perfectly calm. The disciples looked at one another and
said, "What kind of man is this? Even the wind and the

sea obey him!" (Matt. 8:27). Well, since Jesus created the water and the waves and even the Sea of Galilee itself, for that matter, calming them was no big deal for Him. After all, Jesus is God, and God is powerful! Check out this amazing story in Matthew 8:23–27 in the New Testament.

What's God like?

Part 2

> Jesus stretched out his hand and placed it on the leper saying, "Of course I want to. Be clean!" And at once [the man] was clear of the leprosy.
>
> Matthew 8:3 PHILLIPS

In the last chapter, we saw that God is powerful. Powerful enough to calm a storm with just a word. But besides being powerful, God is also really personal. He knows all about you—even what you're thinking. He hears you when you pray, and He cares more about you than anything. In Matthew 8:1–4, Jesus does one of the most up-close-and-personal acts of His entire time on earth. There's this guy who had leprosy, a nerve and skin disease that was killing him. It was so bad that nobody would even get close to a person with that disease back then because they were afraid they would catch it. That had to be one lonely guy. But when Jesus came by, the man said to Him, "If you want to, you can make me clean" (Matt. 8:2 PHILLIPS). In other words, I know you *can* heal me, but I'm not sure you'd want to. "Of course I want to," Jesus said as He reached out and touched the man (Matt. 8:3 PHILLIPS). Instantly, the man was healed. Jesus did what no other person would do.

He got close to and even touched the guy with the dreaded disease. From this story, we see that not only is God powerful but He's also personal. He's big and strong enough to take care of any problem we could ever face, and He's personal enough to care about every detail of our lives.

What about you? Is there something going on in your life that you can tell God about? Go ahead, let Him know. He cares about you and really wants to help you.

What are some things that God could help you with right now? Write them down, then ask God to help you with each one. He loves when we share our lives with Him.

....

....

....

13

What's God's favorite thing?

This is what the Lord of heaven's armies says: "Whoever hurts you hurts what is precious to me."

Zechariah 2:8

This is an easy question to answer. You want to know God's favorite thing in the entire universe? It's YOU! Even though God created the Pacific Ocean and Utah and the Grand Canyon and the Rocky Mountains and India, His favorite thing He ever made is you. In fact, God thinks of you as His special treasure. You're His masterpiece. And even though God can do anything and everything, and He loves what He's created, still His very favorite creation is you. He knows every hair on your head, what kind of ice cream is your favorite, and even how many freckles you have on your nose! Or not on your nose! God loves you so much, and His greatest wish is to be best friends with you.

14

If God is good, why does bad stuff happen?

We know that in everything God works for the good of those who love him.

Romans 8:28

At the very beginning of time, God created the world, and it was perfect. There were no hurt feelings, no sickness, no pain. Everybody got along, and people could talk to God just like they were talking to a friend. And get this: Nobody ever died! But when Adam and Eve, the first people God created, disobeyed Him, their actions did two things: They broke their relationship with God, and they invited evil into the world. Now even nature is messed up. We have hurricanes and fires and all kinds of natural disasters. And because God has given us the freedom to make choices for our lives, people end up hurting one another. People also get sick, and sometimes even die from it, but that was never God's original plan for all of us. Whew. Sounds bad, huh? Yeah, but the good news is there's good news. And God has a plan to bring us all back to Him. And sometimes it's the hard stuff, like pain, sickness, and loss, that opens us up to getting closer to God. Always remember that God is in control of everything, and He wants only the best for us, even when things are hard.

And here's another thought: There may be thousands of times God does protect us from bad stuff and we never even find out about it.

Write God a note telling Him of the hard things you're going through or thanking Him for the good things that are happening right now.

....

....

....

....

....

....

....

....

TALK IT OVER

Good God, Bad Stuff

Sometimes when bad things happen to us, we may think God doesn't care about us. But that's not the truth! He knows what's going on and wants us to ask Him for help.

1. According to this chapter, why does God allow bad stuff to happen?

2. What are some things going on around you that you wish were different?

3. Can you tell about a time when God used hard stuff in your life to bring you closer to Him or to get to know Him better? What was going on, and how did it work out?

4. How does God want us to respond when we're going through hard things?

Close by spending some time in prayer for one another. Share with others some needs that you have and let them pray for you.

Will there be animals in heaven?

Cows and bears will eat together in peace.
Their young will lie down together.

Isaiah 11:7

That's a good question. For one thing, when God created people, He made it clear that we're really different from animals. People aren't just a different kind of animal but an entirely different kind of being. God even said we're made in His image, meaning we can think and love and communicate in ways that animals can't. But God also placed animals (in fact, a lot of them!) in the perfect world He created for Adam and Eve. It was called the garden of Eden, and it was located in the Middle East, in modern-day Iraq. And it was loaded with animals! How do we know that? Because God asked Adam to name them all (Gen. 2:19).

So, since there were animals in God's perfect creation, it seems logical that there will be animals in heaven too. Heaven is a place where we'll have perfect happiness, and if our pets and animals bring us happiness, there's a good chance they'll be there.

And here's an interesting verse—check it out: Isaiah 11:6 (in the Old Testament) says, "In that day the wolf and the lamb will lie down together, and the leopard and goats will be at peace. Calves and fat cattle will be safe among lions, and a little child shall lead them all" (TLB). Most people believe this verse is about when Jesus comes back and rules the world, which will be perfect again. And it could be that this verse is just a poetic description of how perfect the world is going to be, but what if it's not? What if there really are leopards and goats, cattle and lions? I'd like to think that, yes, there will be animals in heaven.

Draw a picture of your pet or, if you don't have a pet, draw an animal you'd like to own, like a cheetah, a red panda, or a blue whale.

DID YOU KNOW?

When Moses was born, there was a law from Pharaoh, the ruler of Egypt, that all newborn Hebrew boys were to be killed. Moses's mother saved his life by placing him in a little basket and putting him into the Nile River. The word used for his basket is the Hebrew word for *ark*. The same word used for the boat Noah built. Interesting, huh?

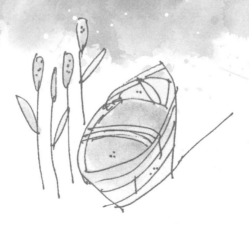

16

Does God really love everyone? Even if they don't believe in Him?

But Christ died for us while we were still sinners. In this way God shows his great love for us.

Romans 5:8

This is a hard one to understand, but the answer is YES, absolutely. Because we're human, we sometimes find it hard to love or even like somebody who's always mean to us or hurts us in any way. But God is perfect. He understands the reasons behind our bad behavior and loves us anyway.

Sometimes people have been hurt in life or think that God has deserted them, so they don't want to have anything to do with Him. But God still loves and cares about all people, even those who don't want to follow Him or who might not believe in Him. In fact, sometimes it's the people who really don't want to think about God who end up meeting Him and loving Him too! Isn't that cool?

TALK IT OVER

God Loves People Who Don't Love Him

God is pretty amazing. He loves not only the people who follow Him but even the ones who don't want to. How does He do that?

1. Can you think of someone in your life who is hard to love?

2. How do you suppose God loves someone who really doesn't like or care about Him?

3. Why does God love people who don't like Him?

4. What's one way you might begin to love someone you don't like?

17

Can we make God sad or upset?

They turned against God so often in the desert!
There they made him very sad.

Psalm 78:40

This goes with the last question. No matter how many bad things we do or how much we disobey God, He never stops loving us. But when we're doing things that hurt us or other people—our mom and dad, our brothers and sisters, or our teachers and friends—it makes God sad. Not because He's mad at us but because He knows that our bad actions aren't good for us or the people around us. He'll never give up on us, but our bad choices sometimes keep us from enjoying the best that God has for us. On the other hand, there are things we can do that make God smile!

What are some ways you can follow God and make Him smile? (Hint: Be nice to a lonely person, obey your parents, or do a kind thing for someone without being asked.)

....

....

....

....

....

....

....

....

....

....

....

18

How much does God love me?

For God loved the world so much that he gave his only Son. God gave his Son so that whoever believes in him may not be lost, but have eternal life.

John 3:16

This is one of those questions that, even if we start to figure it out, there's still no way we could ever fully understand. How much does God love us? It's like if you took a glass of water out of the Pacific Ocean and said, "Is this how much water there is in the ocean?" Or if you took a big breath in and said, "Is this how much air there is in the world?" But God *does* love you more than you'll ever know. As an example, He gave up His own Son, Jesus, to die in your place so you could be friends with God. Jesus Himself said, "The greatest love is shown when a person lays down his life for his friends" (John 15:13 TLB). So, rather than living without you, God proved His love by having Jesus become a person and come to earth so we could get to know God. He lived a perfect life, then went to the cross and died for you and me so we could be forgiven and become God's kids. That's some awesome, gigantic love!

What about dinosaurs? Did they really exist?

> Look at Behemoth.
>> I made him just as I made you.
>> He eats grass like an ox. . . .
> His tail extends like a cedar tree.
>> Job 40:15, 17

Did dinosaurs exist in the garden of Eden, along with Adam and Eve? Or did they go on the ark with Noah and his family? Yikes! What would that have been like? While the Bible isn't really clear specifically about dinosaurs (the word *dinosaur* didn't even exist until 1820), there are a few clues that might make us think there were dinosaurs around with Noah, Adam and Eve, and even a guy in the Bible named Job.

1. Let's start with Adam and Eve. Genesis 1:24–25 says that God made all the land animals on day six of creation. Since we know from fossils found all over the world that dinosaurs existed, we have

to believe that God created them along with the cows, wolves, beavers, and mice.

2. Since God told Noah to take two each of all the animals onto the ark with him, it follows that he would have taken a couple dinosaurs too. They were probably young ones who wouldn't take up too much room. Did you know that some dinosaurs were about the size of a dog? And remember, any of the dinosaurs outside the ark when the flood came would have been swept away. That's probably why we find their fossils in layers of dirt all over the globe.

3. Here's a really cool thing about the possibility of dinosaurs being mentioned in the Bible. In the book of Job (which rhymes with *robe*), there's a creature mentioned that sure sounds a lot like a brontosaurus. According to the description in Job

40:15–22 of this big creature that's called "one of the first of God's works," it "eats grass like an ox," has strength in his body, has bones that "are like tubes of bronze metal," and—check this out—has a tail "like a cedar tree" (a cedar tree is tall and thick). This could be describing a crocodile. Or was it a dinosaur, like a brontosaurus, that these verses are talking about? Could be.

Later, dinosaurs died out. That might have been because of their lack of food or lack of a good environment in which to live. Now all we have are fossil bones of the now-extinct dinosaurs.

Draw a picture of your favorite dinosaur or your favorite animal.

20

What about other religions? Are they the same as believing in Jesus?

Jesus answered, "I am the way. And I am the truth and the life. The only way to the Father is through me."

John 14:6

It can be really confusing when somebody you know says all religions are the same. "We all believe in the same god," they might say. But that's not really true. All other religions are different from Christianity. The biggest difference between the Christian faith and all other religions is . . . Jesus! Other religions teach their followers to do certain things in order to try to reach God. They teach that people need to do good things, live a certain way, and follow certain rules to get near Him. But the good news—no, the *great* news—about Christianity is that God isn't waiting for us to reach *Him*; He's already reached down to us! He knows we can't live a good enough life to get to heaven, so He sent Jesus to live a perfect life and die in our place so we could begin a friendship with God through Jesus. All we have to do is believe. Believe that Jesus is God's Son. And realize that the bad stuff we do, say, and think keeps us away from God. But now Jesus has taken the punishment for us, and we can get close to God again. So we need to thank Him and learn to follow Him. Jesus did it all!

Only Jesus?

Some people think all religions are the same. But Jesus didn't say that. Remember the Bible verse we just read, John 14:6? Keep that in mind as you discuss these questions:

1. What's the difference between following Jesus and other religions?
2. God came down in human form to show us what He's like. How is that different from other religions?
3. What did Jesus do or say that made Him different from other world religions' leaders?

Pray for God to show Himself to you this week.

21

How do I know for sure that God exists?

Anyone who comes to God must believe that he is real
and that he rewards those who truly want to find him.

Hebrews 11:6

While sometimes it's really hard to figure out or understand God because He's so GINORMOUS, He's given us lots of things in this beautiful world that show us who He is. Beautiful locations like the Oregon Coast in the Northwest or the Grand Canyon in Arizona give us a glimpse of the bigness and beauty of God. The Rocky Mountains and the Great Lakes are all incredible places, and as you look at them, you realize that none of them could have come about by accident. They were beautifully designed. Somebody must have created them. Or look at your hand or your eye (you'll need a mirror to do that), and you can appreciate how amazing your body is.

Even though we can't see God or hear Him out loud, He's placed in each of us a sense or feeling that somebody a lot bigger than we are is taking care of us and the whole world (see Rom. 1:19–20 TLB).

Also, it's good to remember all the great things God's done for you during your lifetime. God has kept you safe, helped you heal when you got sick or hurt, and given you good friends and family who love you.

One of the things God loves most about us is when we believe in Him even though we don't see Him. Check out what Jesus said to His disciple Thomas: "You believe because you have seen me. But blessed are those who haven't seen me and believe anyway" (John 20:29 TLB). So don't worry if you have doubts or wonder if God really does exist. He does exist, He's good, and He knows how hard it is to believe in Him sometimes.

God, are you really there?

Believe Even When You Can't See

Has anyone ever told you a story that sounded too un-believable to be real? Some of Jesus's friends felt that way about Him sometimes.

1. Do you ever find it hard to believe that God is real when you can't see Him?

2. What are some ways that God shows us who He is? (Hint: nature, our bodies, how our insides can sense that there's something bigger than us.)

3. If you had been one of Jesus's disciples, would you have been more like John, who believed right away, or Thomas, who needed to see Jesus to believe in Him? Check out the differences in John 20:8 and John 20:25.

4. What are some good things God's done for you in the past?

Pray that God will help you grow in your friendship and trust in Him.

Can God help me when I'm nervous?

Do not worry about anything. But pray and ask God for everything you need. And when you pray, always give thanks.

Philippians 4:6

Sometimes when we feel nervous or even scared about something, we might feel like we're letting God down or like we're not believing in Him enough. Did you know there were people in the Bible who were also really nervous? Moses was afraid to go talk to the king of Egypt. Gideon was nervous about facing his enemies, the Midianites. Queen Esther was afraid to go into the king's court and face him, and Peter became afraid the night Jesus was arrested. So don't feel bad if you're scared of something coming up: moving to a new house, a test at school, or trying out for a team. Sometimes listening to the news can be scary, but if you find yourself feeling nervous, you can do just what all these Bible heroes did.

1. Admit you're scared. Tell God what's making you nervous and ask Him to help you through it. He helped Moses face Pharaoh, Gideon defeat the Midianites, and Esther save the Jewish people. He'll help you with whatever you're facing too!

2. Remember that everybody gets nervous about some things, even adults. Most people might not show it or admit it, but we all get scared of some of the things that happen in our lives.

3. If your anxiety is really bothering you, you might need to talk to someone about it. Tell your parents, a friend, or your Sunday school teacher what you're feeling. They'll probably have some good advice for you.

Where does God live?

This is what the Lord says:

"The skies are my throne.
 The earth is my footstool.
So do you think you can build a house for me?"

Isaiah 66:1

Good question. You might hear that God lives:

  A. In heaven
  B. Everywhere
  C. Inside your heart
  D. All of the above

You want the answer? It's D. All of these are true! Yes, God does live in heaven, everywhere, and inside of all the people who are friends with Him. That's because God lives . . . are you ready for this? . . . OUTSIDE OF TIME AND SPACE! He's transcendent! (Remember question 2?)

Because we're people, and we and everything we know—pets, plants, buildings—all exist in time and space, it's hard for us to understand that God doesn't live there and isn't limited by them. He can be everywhere at any time He wants. There's a big word for that, it's called *omnipresent*, and it means He can be everywhere at once. Cool, huh? Yeah. Hard to understand? Totally.

Everywhere at Once

Use the word *omnipresent* in front of your parents. *Omnipresent* means "everywhere at once." Since God isn't a person with a body, He can be everywhere at the same time, or omnipresent. Try out that word sometime today. Your parents will be really impressed.

24

Why did God create mosquitoes?

So God made the wild animals, the tame animals and all the small crawling animals to produce more of their own kind. God saw that this was good.

Genesis 1:25

Mosquitoes can be really annoying if you think about it. Especially if you've been bitten by one while you were camping or even in your own backyard. When God created the world, He said that everything was good (Gen. 1:31), and apparently mosquitoes were part of His plan. Yuck! But some people believe that when God originally created mosquitoes, they didn't bite people. Like bees, they got their food from plants and nectar. But when Adam and Eve disobeyed God, everything in the world went topsy-turvy. That means upside down. Even some of the good things God created went bad after that. And quite possibly, that may have been when mosquitoes started biting people! So yeah, God created mosquitoes, but they were probably a nicer bunch back at the beginning.

25

Does God sleep?

He who guards Israel
never rests or sleeps.
Psalm 121:4

The Bible says that God never sleeps. He never gets tired, and He doesn't ever nod off from carefully watching over all of us. Since He's not a human, God never needs to take a nap. Sometimes you might feel as if you're all alone and that God is either gone or asleep. But that's not true. Psalm 121:3–4 says, "He will not let you be defeated. He who guards you never sleeps. He who guards Israel never rests or sleeps." So you can always be sure that God is watching you and won't miss a thing.

Asleep in the Storm

"But wait! I thought Jesus fell asleep in the boat. If He's God, why did He need to sleep?" Such a great question! Yes, according to Mark 4:38, Jesus was asleep in the back of the boat when the storm came up. And the disciples had to wake Him up! The reason Jesus was asleep, or tired for that matter, was that when Jesus was on earth, He was not only totally God but totally human. He got sleepy, hungry, sad, and all other kinds of feelings, just like us, because He was human too.

God? You awake?

26

Why did God rest on the seventh day of creation? Was He tired?

By the seventh day God finished the work he had been doing. So on the seventh day he rested from all his work.

Genesis 2:2

Genesis 2:2 says that God rested on the seventh day (and He wants us to do the same), but He didn't rest because He was tired. He rested because He was all done creating everything. In fact, the Hebrew word for "rest" in this passage is *shabbat*, which can mean "to stop" or "to cease." So, the verse might read "God *stopped* when He was done creating." The phrase also might indicate that He was pleased and satisfied with what He'd done. Even though God never gets tired or needs to sleep, He knows we're different from Him and we get tired and need rest. So God wants us to take at least one day a week to relax and restore. Most people take Sunday off, which works out great because that's the day most people go to church to learn about God. Taking a day off, or a Sabbath, not only gives us rest but it shows that we're trusting God to help us finish the work we need to do.

What are some chores you do around the house to help your family?

....

....

....

....

....

....

....

....

....

DID YOU KNOW?

Where did life on earth begin? Well, according to Genesis 2 in the Old Testament, it began in the garden of Eden, in what we now know as Iraq. In the Scriptures, four rivers are mentioned, only two of which exist today—the Tigris and the Euphrates. They travel through Iraq and end up in the Persian Gulf. So, somewhere between those two rivers was the site of the garden of Eden, God's paradise on earth.

Can we see God?

No one has ever seen God. But if we love each other, God lives in us.

1 John 4:12

This is a great question! If God is real, why can't we see Him? It's really hard to believe in someone we can't see or touch. The main reason we can't see God is that He is a spirit. God doesn't have a physical body like you do. So how do we know He's real if we can't see Him? Well, think about this: The wind is real, but we can't see it either. And gravity is real. If you drop a pencil, it'll go down, not up, right? That's gravity! And even though we can't see gravity, we know it's real. So just because we can't see God doesn't mean He's not real. He's there, all right.

By the way, there is one way you can see God, and that's by looking at Jesus! Colossians 1:15 says that "Christ is the exact likeness of the unseen God" (TLB). In other words, even though we can't see the invisible God, when we read about Jesus in the Bible, we get a good glimpse of God and what He's like.

Can Christians hear God talking to them?

Speak, Lord. I am your servant, and I am listening.

1 Samuel 3:9

The number one thing on God's to-do list is to be friends with each one of us. And what do friends do? They talk to one another! But you won't hear God's actual voice very often. There might be a really rare time when somebody actually hears God's voice (He is God after all; He can do whatever He wants), but usually we hear God in different ways:

1. We hear what He has to say by reading the Bible. This book is God's Word, or love letter, to us. As we read it and get to know it, we discover who God is and how much He loves us. The Bible is full of stories of people who knew God, and most of them followed Him the best they could. By reading about these people, we can learn a lot about what it means to trust God and follow Him.

2. We hear God by listening to our church leaders, pastors, and teachers. These people have known God for a long time, so they can teach us about Him. God uses them to give His messages to us.

3. And finally, God might speak to you by giving you a thought in your mind. Sometimes God will speak to us directly through His Spirit, who lives inside us. When you feel like God has told you something, make sure you talk with an older Christian—maybe your mom or dad—about what you think God has said to you to make sure it really is God speaking. And make sure that what you heard goes along with what the Bible says. If, for example, you think God told you to hit your little brother, nah, that's probably not God speaking.

TALK IT OVER

Hearing God

Sometimes it's hard to hear what God's saying to us because we don't usually hear an actual voice.

1. Talking to a friend is easy. Why is it harder to talk to God?
2. Why can it be so hard to hear from God?
3. According to this chapter, what are some ways we can hear from God?
4. Can you think of a time when you felt like God spoke to you? It might have been a thought, a sermon, or something you read in your Bible.

Take some time to pray for one another. Ask God to help you listen to Him and get to know Him better.

29

Was Jesus a real person?

The first book I wrote was about everything that Jesus did and taught.

Acts 1:1

This is a really good question. Some people think that Jesus and the Bible were just made up to teach us how to live and be good. But the writers of the Bible never said that. They constantly talked about Jesus doing certain things: healing people, teaching, eating, and going to parties. They mentioned real places He visited, like Jerusalem, Nazareth, and Capernaum, and real people He talked to, like Zacchaeus, Peter, King Herod, and John the Baptist.

But other writers, people who didn't even follow Jesus, wrote about Him too. A Roman historian named Tacitus wrote about a man named Jesus, who was punished and executed by Pontius Pilate during the rule of Emperor Tiberius. That's exactly what the Bible says! And another Jewish historian named Josephus wrote about Jesus and the cool things He did and about how His followers called Him the Messiah, the Anointed One.

Plus, in the past few decades, archaeologists have dug up things that refer to people mentioned in the Bible. So, most of the people who study this stuff agree that Jesus really did exist.

30

What was Jesus's last name?

The followers said, "It is about Jesus of Nazareth. He was a prophet from God to all the people. He said and did many powerful things."

Luke 24:19

Have you ever thought about that? After all, we all have last names that usually identify us with our families. Your last name might be Smith or Jonas or Snodgrass. But Jesus didn't have a last name. Back then, most people didn't have last names. They might have been identified by who their father was, like James son of Zebedee or Bartimaeus, which means "the son of Timaeus." Some might have had a nickname, like Simon the Zealot (which meant someone who was radically committed to opposing Rome at that time), or even been identified by where they lived, like Mary Magdalene. Magdala was a town by the Sea of Galilee and was where Mary grew up. Lots of people referred to Jesus as Jesus of Nazareth since that was where He was raised.

Since people know the name Jesus Christ, a lot of them think that Christ was His last name. But the word *Christ* comes from a Greek word that means "anointed one" or "savior." Actually, it would be better to say Jesus *the* Christ. Jesus the Anointed One, the One who saves us.

Jesus's Name

Jesus's name itself means "savior" and is the Greek word for the Hebrew name Joshua. There was a man named Joshua who led his people into the promised land a long time ago. You can find his story in the Old Testament book Joshua, named after him.

Did Jesus have any brothers and sisters?

He is only the son of the carpenter. And his mother is Mary. His brothers are James, Joseph, Simon and Judas. And all his sisters are here with us.

Matthew 13:55–56

While some people believe that Jesus was an only child (I mean, He was pretty special when you think about it), the New Testament clearly mentions that Jesus had not only brothers but sisters as well. Matthew 13:55–56 mentions His brothers and sisters. The brothers' names were James, Joseph, Simon, and Judas (not the Judas who betrayed Jesus—that was another guy).

Sisters are mentioned too, but they aren't mentioned by name. So yes, Jesus lived in a family a lot like yours! Since Jesus was the Son of God, and Mary was His mother, these other kids were half brothers and sisters to Jesus. Their mom was Mary, but their dad was Joseph. Jesus's dad is God.

Draw a picture of your family. What is one of your favorite things about each person?

32

Did Jesus get along with His brothers and sisters?

[Jesus] was tempted in every way that we are, but he did not sin.

Hebrews 4:15

There's not much in the Bible about Jesus as a young boy—except one story of Him at twelve years old getting left behind at the temple when His family headed home. But since we know that Jesus was perfect in every way—the way He thought, talked, and acted—we know that He never did anything to hurt or put down His brothers or sisters. But did they get along with Him? Not all the time.

When Jesus was about thirty years old, He began to travel around teaching people about God and even told them that God was His Father. His brothers didn't believe Him and even thought Jesus was crazy! (Check it out in Mark 3:21.) They wanted to take Him home before He got into trouble. But later on, after Jesus died and was raised from the dead, some of His brothers joined the disciples and followed Him. One of His brothers, James, even became a leader in the early church!

Brothers and Sisters

In many ways, Jesus grew up and lived just like all of us. Including living with brothers and sisters!

1. We found out that Jesus did have brothers and sisters. How do you think they all got along?

2. Did you know that Jesus never did anything wrong? Even when His brothers and sisters might have bugged Him? How hard do you think that was for Him?

3. Has your brother or sister ever done anything to bother you? Be honest.

4. Have you ever done anything that's bugged your brother or sister? Be really honest! Do you need to ask forgiveness for something you've done or said?

5. What are some ways we can follow God and show His love to our brothers and sisters?

Take a few moments and pray for one another. Tell someone in your family you love them and are thankful for them.

Did Jesus really cry?

Jesus cried.
John 11:35

Yes, the Bible tells us that Jesus cried two different times:

1. When Jesus's good friend Lazarus died, Jesus cried. Why did He cry? Because Jesus looked around and saw all of Lazarus's friends and family hurting big-time. Jesus gets sad when people are going through a hard time. And losing their friend Lazarus was really hard. Here's the good news: Four days after Lazarus died, Jesus raised him from the dead! Check it out in John 11.

2. The second time Jesus cried was when He saw how the people of Israel were rejecting Him. After He came into Jerusalem, their capital city, Jesus cried because He knew that the people who were welcoming Him that day were soon going to desert Him (Luke 19:41). He also knew that Israel's enemies were going to come and attack them

in a few years and Jerusalem would be destroyed. You can read about this in Luke 13:34–35.

Jesus might have cried more often than that, but the Gospel writers didn't write it down. When Jesus, God's Son, became a person, a man, He experienced all the feelings that we do. He laughed and joked, He cried, He got tired, and He felt rejected by His friends. Isn't it nice to know that Jesus knows how we feel when we laugh, cry, get tired, or feel left out by our friends?

Why did Jesus do miracles?

> When Jesus arrived, he saw a large crowd. He felt sorry for them and healed those who were sick.
>
> Matthew 14:14

This question actually has three answers:

1. Jesus sometimes did a miracle in order to prove who He was. I mean, when you go around telling people you're the Son of God, they might want a little proof. So, by doing miracles, like healing diseases, feeding five thousand people with a couple fish and loaves, turning water into wine, and even raising someone from the dead, Jesus proved He was who He said He was! If Jesus was really God in human form, then miracles like these would be easy for Him. In fact, some people believed in Jesus *because* of His miracles.

2. Sometimes Jesus did a miracle because it was the best thing to do at that moment. A good example of this would be the time He walked on the water.

His friends were out in the middle of the lake in a boat that was being swamped by a storm, and Jesus wanted to reach them. So He broke His own law of nature and walked out to be with them and bring them comfort during a scary time.

3. The Bible says that the number one reason Jesus did miracles was because He loved people and cared for them. He had compassion on them, which means He cared deeply for them and their needs. He showed compassion to sick people, to hungry people, and even to scared people. Love does that.

The Miracles of Jesus

Here are some of the cool, miraculous things Jesus did while He was here on earth:

He calmed a storm at sea with a word. (Matt. 8:23–27)
He walked on water to reach His friends. (Mark 6:45–52)
He healed a blind man outside the gates of Jericho. (Mark 10:46–52)
He raised a lady's son from the dead. (Luke 7:11–17)
He healed a man who had been sick for thirty-eight years. (John 5:1–8)

Why did Jesus speak in parables?

Jesus answered, "Only you can know the secret truths about the kingdom of heaven. Other people cannot know these secret truths."

Matthew 13:11

A parable is a story that teaches a lesson. Jesus loved to use parables when He was explaining what God's kingdom was like. He told stories about sheep and goats, wheat and weeds, missing coins and mustard seeds. But why did He use parables? He knew there was no way we could understand the kingdom of God without Him trying to make it easier for us. Sometimes Jesus used parables or stories to make things clearer to the people who were listening to Him. For example, when He told the story of the good Samaritan, He showed us how we can love and take care of people, even if they're different from us. And when He spoke about the son who ran away from home, He was teaching a lesson about God's forgiveness and how He welcomes all of us back, no matter what we've done.

But other times, Jesus said He used stories so that some people *wouldn't* understand what He was talking about. What? Why would He do that? Even though Jesus loves everyone and wants them to know Him, He knew that by telling parables or stories, like the one about the prodigal son or the lost sheep, only the people who really wanted to know Him would dig deeper and ask questions about the stories. Often, Jesus would tell a story, then wait for people to ask Him what it meant. How about you? Did you know that by reading this book, you're digging deeper into understanding God too? Good job!

Why did Jesus always wear a robe?

She was thinking, "If I can touch his coat, then I will be healed."

Matthew 9:21

If you've ever seen a picture of Jesus (it would be a painting; they didn't have cameras two thousand years ago!), He's probably wearing a white robe. You know why? Because that's what everybody wore back then. That was the style. Men wore robes because they were comfortable and protected them from the hot sun in the Middle East. It sometimes gets as hot as 100 degrees during the day in Israel, where Jesus lived! In fact, in a lot of countries in the Middle East today, men still wear long robes and headpieces to protect them from the sun. But Jesus also wore special things on His robe that a rabbi or teacher would wear, like tassels at the bottom. And sometimes He might have had an outer robe that He could use as a blanket if He was sleeping outside.

Since Jesus was a man as well as God, some people think that if He were walking around today, He'd probably be wearing the same style of clothing that everyone else is wearing.

Can Jesus fly?

After he said this, as they were watching, he was lifted up. A cloud hid him from their sight.

Acts 1:9

We never see anywhere in the Bible where Jesus flew before He died and was raised again from the dead. He was just like us, limited by gravity. But Acts 1:9 says that after He died and rose again, Jesus was lifted up to heaven until a cloud covered Him, and the disciples couldn't see Him anymore. That sure sounds like flying to me!

Earlier in Jesus's life, the devil tried to get Him to fly when he took Jesus up to the top of the temple and dared Him to jump off (Matt. 4:5-6). But Jesus refused and said, "Do not test the Lord your God" (Matt. 4:7). Now, Jesus could do a lot of cool things after He rose from the dead. Like He could come through locked doors and appear and disappear whenever He wanted. But He wasn't a ghost or a spirit. His disciples touched Him, and He could sit down and eat food with them too! But Jesus is God, so if He wanted to fly, I suppose He could.

DID YOU KNOW?

The Bible was written over two thousand years ago, and yet it still speaks to us today. One of the ways it speaks to us is through some of the phrases we use every day that first started in God's Word. Check these out and see if any of them sound familiar:

"By the Skin of My Teeth"

This means you just barely escaped something. Like "I got out of there by the skin of my teeth." This phrase comes from the Old Testament book of Job, chapter 19, verse 20. There it says, "I am nothing but skin and bones. I have escaped with only the skin of my teeth."

"A Drop in the Bucket"

This usually means a really small amount, like "A thousand dollars is just a drop in the bucket for that billionaire over there." This phrase comes from Isaiah 40:15, which says, "The nations are like one small drop in a bucket. They are no more than the dust on [God's] measuring scales. To him the islands are no more than fine dust on his scales."

"A Wolf in Sheep's Clothing"

This phrase usually describes a sneaky person who looks good on the outside but isn't good on the inside. Think about it: If you were a wolf that wanted to sneak in with the sheep, what would be a perfect disguise? Right, dress like a sheep! In Matthew 7:15, Jesus told His disciples to beware of wolves in sheep's clothing—people who aren't what they appear to be.

Did Jesus ever go to school?

After three days they found him. Jesus was sitting in the Temple with the religious teachers, listening to them and asking them questions.

Luke 2:46

The Bible doesn't mention specifically if Jesus went to school when He was a boy, but we can guess that He did for a couple reasons:

1. For one thing, we know He could read because He stood up in front of the whole synagogue (that was like the Jewish people's church) and read from the Old Testament (Luke 4:16–17). Since He read in front of the whole place, that means someone had taught Jesus how to read.

2. We can also guess that Jesus went to school because when He was growing up, almost all Jewish boys went to school around the age of six or seven. Before that time, His education would have been brought by His mom and dad. They

would have taught Him the Hebrew alphabet and the history of the Jewish people, and they would have read the Scriptures to Him. In Jesus's time, there was just the Old Testament. Most young Jewish boys would have had the first five books of the Old Testament completely memorized by the time they were twelve years old. Whew! When Jesus went to school, He would have learned more about the Scriptures, history, reading and writing, how to treat one another, and perhaps some science and arithmetic.

Jesus received His early education at home where Joseph taught Him to love God with all His heart, soul, and strength. Can you imagine teaching Jesus to love God?

Draw a picture of your school. What do you think Jesus's school looked like?

Did Jesus really walk on water? How did He do that?

At some time between three and six o'clock in the morning, Jesus came to them, walking on the water.

Mark 6:48

Yes! Jesus really did walk on the water in order to reach His friends, the disciples, while they were in a boat in the middle of a storm. Mark 6:46 says that Jesus went up on a hillside to pray after His friends got into a boat and headed to the other side of the Sea of Galilee. After they had rowed for a while, a storm came up and threatened to sink the little boat they were in! Verse 48 says Jesus *saw* them as they struggled to keep the boat afloat. Isn't that cool? He saw them just like He

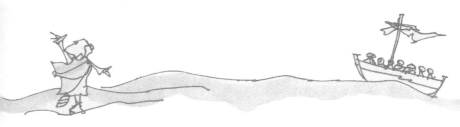

sees you all the time. So He climbed down from the hill, and since He didn't have a boat, He just stepped out and walked all the way to where His friends were. Isn't that great? As for *how* He did it, guess we just have to figure that since Jesus is God and He created the Sea of Galilee back at the beginning of creation, He definitely had the power to walk on it.

Does God still heal people today?

Jesus Christ is the same yesterday, today, and forever.

Hebrews 13:8

The quick answer to this question is YES! Absolutely! Hebrews 13:8 says that Jesus Christ is the same yesterday, today, and forever. This means that because Jesus died and rose from the dead, He's still alive today and doing the same things He did when He was walking around on earth with His disciples. Sometimes God heals in quiet ways or in slow ways that nobody notices. And sometimes He takes a hopeless situation, turns it around, and heals someone in a really cool, miraculous way. Like someone who has cancer but then goes back to the doctor and the cancer has disappeared! There are also stories of people who were in car crashes or other accidents where they might have died but came away without a scratch. God is still working today, and He's still doing amazing things!

There are two things to remember when you or someone you know is sick or hurt:

1. Pray for them! God loves all of us and hurts when one of us is hurting, but He really wants us to get involved and pray for the person who's sick or hurt.

    By the way, God loves to answer our prayers because it helps us grow our faith in Him!

2. When someone you're praying for gets better, make sure you thank the Lord for answering your prayer. He loves when we let Him know how grateful we are that He heard us and answered us. If the person isn't healed yet, keep praying, and thank God that He hears you and wants to help the person, even if it hasn't happened yet.

What if God doesn't heal the person I prayed for?

Just as the heavens are higher than the earth,
so are my ways higher than your ways.
And my thoughts are higher than your
thoughts.

Isaiah 55:9

This is a really good question and one people have struggled with ever since the beginning of time. When God doesn't heal somebody, does it mean I didn't pray right? Or enough? Does God not love the person? Or me? Well, neither God nor the Bible says any of those things. The one thing (and the *biggest* thing) to remember about God is that He's, well, *God*. And He's so much bigger than we'll ever completely know or understand. He knows exactly what every person needs and what's best for them. There are some things we won't ever understand until we're in heaven with Him. So, does that mean we should just give up praying for people? No, not at all. Even if God doesn't answer our prayers for a certain person the way we want Him to, God wants us to keep praying and believing that He hears us.

Two things to remember when God doesn't heal someone you're praying for:

1. Let God know how you're feeling. Let Him know if you're disappointed, sad, or even mad. It's okay. He wants you to be honest with Him and let Him know what you're feeling.
2. Keep praying. Don't let this make you lose faith. Remember, God is on your side, and He wants the best for you and the person you're praying for. Remembering that is part of learning to trust Him. It's hard, but God is always there for you and always has your best in mind.

Is there someone you can pray for right now?

. . . .

. . . .

. . . .

. . . .

. . . .

Are You Listening, God?

Even though God loves it when we talk to Him, He doesn't always answer us the way we want Him to. But He always knows what's best for us.

1. Can you think of a time when you prayed for something or someone and God answered it right away? Share about it.

2. Can you think of a time when God took a really long time to answer your prayer about something? Looking back, can you see now why He might have waited to answer?

3. Why do you think God sometimes doesn't answer our prayers or waits a long time to answer them?

4. Is there something right now you're praying for and you still don't see God's answer?

This would be a great time to pray for those things that seem impossible right now. But remember, nothing is impossible for God!

Is it okay to go to the doctor or take medicine when I'm sick, or should I just pray?

I am the Lord who heals you.
Exodus 15:26

One thing Jesus said while He was here on earth was "Seek first the kingdom of God" (Matt. 6:33 ESV). That means we should put God ahead of anything else in our lives. So, if you get sick or hurt and need medical care, that's fine. Go for it! If you are able and have time to when you're sick or hurt, you can "seek God first" by praying. Ask Him to help you and heal you. He might do so in one of three ways:

1. He might heal you instantly. God has done that before, and He'll continue to do that. When He does heal you like that, make sure you thank Him!

2. He might heal you naturally. Aren't you glad God made your body so that it can heal itself? Like when you cut your finger, it'll heal back up in a few days. That's cool. Or if you get sick, you usually get over it in a few days. That's another way God heals you.

3. He might heal you with the help of a doctor or medicine. God creates some people to be very smart and to want to help people get better through medicine, so they become doctors, nurses, and medical technicians. You can be thankful for them too, because God uses them to help people get better.

Remember, God is our best doctor, and He might use any of these ways to make us better. So if you're sick or hurt, tell God about it, and if you need to, go see a doctor and get better!

Why should we go to church if God is everywhere?

You should not stay away from the church meetings, as some are doing. But you should meet together and encourage each other.

Hebrews 10:25

While it's true that God is everywhere and with us all the time, He still wants us to go to church whenever we can. Even though you can be best friends with God all by yourself, He created us to be with and around other people who love Him and who love us. Our family, friends, and other people who know God and are growing in their friendship with Him can really help us grow closer to God too. Also, when we go to church, we get a chance to worship Him and learn more about Him through our pastors, Sunday school teachers, and others. Plus, when you go to church or Sunday school, who knows—you might end up being an encourager to someone else!

Four Ways to Grow in Your Friendship with God

If you want to grow in your friendship with God, there are four things you can do right now to get started.

1. **Read your Bible every day.** Even if you read for only five minutes a day, you'll start to learn more about God, Jesus, and lots of God's people and how they lived and learned to trust God.

2. **Talk to God.** We already talked about prayer. Just talk to God every day. Let Him know how you're doing, how you're feeling, the great stuff going on in your life, and the hard stuff. He really wants to know, and by talking to Him every day, you'll start to get to know Him better too.

3. **Get together with other Jesus followers.** The best way to do this is by going to church, Sunday school, or a youth group. You might start a small group with friends who meet at your house after school to pray and read the Bible. It's important to be around people who love God and who love you.

4. **Start serving.** Find simple ways you can help other people. You might smile at a neighbor, be nice to the new kid in school, or even surprise a friend with cupcakes. How about cleaning your room without being asked? Or taking out the trash? There are a bunch of ways you can serve others. Can you think of some other ways?

How does God hear all our prayers at once?

I was in trouble. So I called to the Lord.
The Lord answered me and set me free.
Psalm 118:5

This is one of those great questions that kids—*and* adults—ask. After all, when we're talking to someone, we can focus on only one, two, or maybe three people at the same time. But did you know that there are billions of people around the world who pray every day, and God hears every single one of them? I guess the best answer to how He can do that is that God lives outside of time. In fact, He *created* time. Remember question 2, "How old is God?" Since God created time and somehow lives outside of it, get ready—He can hear everyone's prayers at once! Remember, we're not just talking about some super guy here; we're talking about the God who created the stars, the sun, the moon, and even time itself. Whew. So, since He can be everywhere at once and in every *time* at once, He can hear and answer all our prayers.

TALK IT OVER

How Does God Know Each One of Us?

Since we're just people, sometimes we get a really small idea of who God is. But He is so much bigger, stronger, and more amazing than we can even imagine. And He's so much more personal than we realize too.

1. Do you have a best friend? What do you like about them?
2. If you could tell God anything at all, what would it be?
3. How do you feel when you hear that God knows everything about you? Nervous? Happy? Excited?
4. Jesus tells us that God is the perfect Father who knows us, loves us, and wants only good things for us. What are some cool things God's done for you?

Does God laugh?

And Sarah said, "God has made me laugh. Everyone who hears about this will laugh with me."

Genesis 21:6

Do you like to laugh? I think we all do. And the Bible says that we're created in God's image. That doesn't mean we look like God, but it does mean that we have a lot of the same qualities He has. We can love, figure things out, solve problems, feel sad, or, yeah . . . feel happy! Also, since we know that when we look at Jesus, we see God the Father, we just need to check out what Jesus does. While we don't see anywhere in the Bible where Jesus specifically laughs, we can see His sense of humor in a lot of what He says. He talks about a camel going through the eye of a needle and a log sticking out of somebody's eye! Even though a lot of people seem to think that Jesus was serious all the time, I don't think so. Since Jesus experienced all the same feelings we experience, we can be sure that, yes, He did laugh!

Does God cry?

Listen to my cry for help.
My king and my God, I pray to you.

Psalm 5:2

God does cry and feel sad, especially when we're doing things that hurt ourselves or others. Since Father God is a spirit, He probably doesn't actually cry tears, but the Bible is clear that He feels sadness whenever His kids (that's you!) are hurting. It's hard to understand, but somehow God knows everything we're going through and everything we're feeling. So, if you're feeling sad, scared, or lonely, let Him know about it. He understands. And He wants to help.

And of course Jesus, who is God in human form, cried a couple times during His life. We talked about the times that Jesus cried in question 33.

Did God create the internet?

I have given him the skill, ability and knowledge to do all kinds of work.

Exodus 31:3

This is an interesting question! And it's safe to say that the answer would be yes, but like so many other things in our lives, God did it in a very different way. He used people to create the internet. God gives some people special skills and abilities to do amazing things for Him and for other people. Aren't you glad He gave some people the ability to be doctors or soldiers or teachers or veterinarians (the people who take care of our pets)? Well, He also gave some people the ability to dream of and then create computers, laptops, and even the internet. These are some pretty smart people! God loves it when we use the gifts, talents, and abilities He's given us to create things that help people and bring attention to Him.

What are some of your special talents and abilities? Sports? Art? Music? Being a good friend? List three of them here:

....

....

....

How can you use these talents to help other people get to know God?

....

....

....

....

....

....

....

....

48

Did God create the food chain?

So will every animal that crawls on the ground and every fish in the sea respect and fear you.

Genesis 9:2

In case you're wondering what the food chain is, it basically means that out in nature, bigger animals eat smaller ones. For example, a killer whale might eat a large fish, like a salmon. The salmon might eat a smaller fish, which also eats fish or eggs that are smaller than it. So scientists called this the food chain a long time ago. It's a way that animals live and survive, but it wasn't always the way it is now.

When God created the world and the first people, Adam and Eve, everything was perfect. There was no fear or pain

or big animals eating smaller ones. It appears that people and animals ate only vegetables and fruits back in the garden of Eden. So yes, God did create a kind of food chain at first—with plants.

Since there was no death, people and animals lived forever. But when Adam and Eve rebelled against God and death came into the world, things got really messed up. Suddenly people were fighting and animals were getting killed. In fact, an animal had to die to provide the skins that Adam and Eve wore as clothes after they rebelled against God (Gen. 3:21). Ever since then, people have used animals for food and even clothing. So, since they weren't just eating plants anymore, the food chain changed.

Was there really a big flood during Noah's lifetime?

The water continued to rise until it was more than 20 feet above the mountains.

Genesis 7:20

Yes, there was. And apparently, it happened pretty much the way the Bible tells us. Why do scientists think there really was a flood during Noah's time? Here are two reasons:

1. There are fossils (animal bones from a long time ago that are stuck in layers of ground) that give evidence of a big flood. Some of these are fish bones that have been found a mile above sea level and hundreds of miles from the ocean. How did they get there? Why would there be fish bones up on the side of a mountain that's no-where near the ocean? Probably because at some point that mountain was under water!

2. Another reason to believe the flood really happened is because a number of different people groups all over the world have stories about a huge flood that covered the earth. People as far away from each other as China, Italy, Greece, Mexico, and even Hawaii all have stories of a big flood! And some of the stories even tell about a man and his wife, their sons, and their sons' wives, who escaped the flood on a big boat. Hmm. Who does that sound like?

How did God make rainbows?

I am putting my rainbow in the clouds.
Genesis 9:13

God made the very first rainbow when Noah's ark landed and settled on Mount Ararat after the flood. God wanted to give Noah a sign that He would never flood the whole earth again, so God made a rainbow in the sky. He did this by creating a misty sky (like when we have rain showers) and having the sunlight hit the mist just right. The water in the mist helped break up the sun's rays, and since sunlight is made up of every color, the result was a beautiful, seven-color rainbow! So, every time you see a rainbow after or during a rain shower, you can remember the story of Noah and God's promise—that He'll never again flood the whole world.

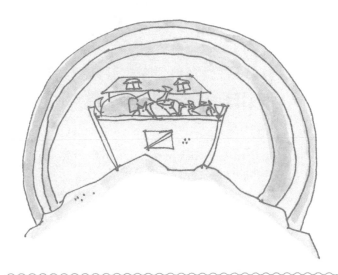

Create Your Own Rainbow!

You can make your own rainbow. It's easy. Just stand with your back to the sun and spray water from a hose into the air. You might need to move it around a bit till it appears, but pretty soon you'll have made your own rainbow!

Did Jonah really get swallowed by a fish?

Jonah was in the stomach of the big fish for three days
and three nights.

Matthew 12:40

Wow, if you haven't read or heard the story of Jonah,
check it out. It's a wild one! It's so crazy, in fact,
that a lot of people think it was made up. Jonah has his
own book in the Old Testament. There it is, right between
Obadiah and Micah. And he's mentioned as a real guy
in 2 Kings 14:25.

So, here's what happened: God wanted Jonah to tell his
enemies, the Assyrians, about God, but Jonah ran away
because he hated the Assyrians. He got on a boat and
headed west, away from Assyria (and, Jonah thought,
away from God!). As he was on the boat, a huge storm
formed and looked like it was going to sink the ship, so
the crew threw Jonah overboard! But God sent a big fish—
maybe a whale—to swallow Jonah so he'd have some time
to think about what he'd done. It was like a time-out for
Jonah. After three days inside the fish, Jonah changed

his mind, the fish spit him out, and Jonah went and told the Assyrians about God.

But did he really get swallowed by a big fish and survive? Why not? Other people have been swallowed by whales and survived. One as recently as 2021. (Don't believe me? Check out his story here: https://www.kids news.com.au/news/man-eaten-by-whale-lives-to-tell -tale/news-story/07678fe06afac66e58c7fff9b4453a0f.) But you know who believed Jonah's story? Jesus! Check it out in Matthew 12:39–41. And think about it: If God is who we think He is, it would be no problem for Him to get a fish to swallow Jonah and for the guy to stay alive in there for three days. So yes, the Jonah story is real.

Why did God create germs?

Let them praise the Lord
   because they were created by his command.

Psalm 148:5

Since we know that God created everything, and since we know that germs exist, we have to believe that God created them too. Ew. Why would He do that? We might never know for sure, but as we get to know God, we learn two things:

1. God never does anything by accident.
2. Everything He ever does is for our good.

Many people believe that when God created germs (or microbes), He did it for our good. Did you know that we've got millions, even billions, of microbes in our bodies right now? But don't worry! Scientists tell us that

some germs do lots of *good* things. They help us digest our food, heal from injuries, and even keep the bad microbes out of our bodies. While some germs do make us sick, God created the good ones to protect us. And could it be that when Adam and Eve disobeyed God, some of the germs that were good suddenly became harmful? Could be.

What's the deal with angels? Who are they and what do they do?

God sent the angel Gabriel to a virgin who lived in Nazareth, a town in Galilee. She was engaged to marry a man named Joseph from the family of David. Her name was Mary.

Luke 1:26

In both the Old Testament and the New Testament, the words used to describe angels mean "messengers," so that must be their main job. An angel named Gabriel appeared to Mary to let her know she was going to be the mother of Jesus. And an angel spoke to Joseph to tell him that Mary was going to have a baby who was going to be the Son of God. After Jesus was born, an angel also warned Joseph in a dream to take Mary and Jesus and escape to Egypt. There are also other angels who are more like warriors and protectors. The Bible says that there are angels all around us and that they're here to help take care of and protect us (Ps. 91:11–12). Angels are cool, but they exist to serve God and they seem to like to be in the background most of the time. The Bible says that we might even meet an angel sometime and not know it (Heb. 13:2).

A Few Things about Angels

1. They're created beings, so they haven't been around forever. But they won't ever die.
2. Angels have different jobs to do. Some protect us, some deliver messages, and some praise and worship God.
3. A lot of people think that when we die, we become angels, but that's not true. In heaven, we'll still be ourselves but in special, brand-new bodies that never get tired or sick or hurt. How cool is that?

What's a guardian angel?

Be careful. Don't think these little children are worth nothing. I tell you that they have angels in heaven who are always with my Father in heaven.

Matthew 18:10

Just like the phrase sounds, a guardian angel is an angel who guards us and protects us. We can't see them, but we know they're there. As I mentioned earlier, we can't see air, but we know it's there too. In Matthew 18:10, Jesus tells us that we're supposed to love, respect, and protect little children because they have angels in heaven (more than one!) who are with God all the time. God gives us angels to protect us and guide us, and sometimes we don't even know it. But we don't ever need to talk to them or pray to them. The only one we need to pray to is God through Jesus, His Son. And if He thinks we need an angel to help us, you can be sure He'll send one.

55

Does God have a name?

Moses said to God, "When I go to the Israelites, I will say to them, 'The God of your ancestors sent me to you.' What if the people say, 'What is his name?' What should I tell them?"

Exodus 3:13

God has a few names that we see in the Bible. The one most of the people in the Old Testament used was YHWH or Yahweh. This name means "to exist or be." That means that God has always been around and He's always with us. Some people use the name Jehovah as the name of God. And sometimes they put that name together with other words to describe parts of who God is. Here are just a few of God's names:

Jehovah Jireh: The Lord my Provider. God will give us everything we need, so we never need to worry.

Jehovah Shalom: The Lord my Peace. *Shalom* is a cool Hebrew word that means more than just "peace." It means "health, rest, well-being, and wholeness." And God gives this gift to us all the time.

Jehovah Sabaoth: The Lord of Armies. This means that God is the general, or leader, of all the angels in heaven. That's pretty powerful!

Jehovah Raah: The Lord my Shepherd. Just as a good shepherd cares for, provides for, and protects his sheep, God wants to do that for all of us every day.

Abba: A Hebrew name for Father, Dad, or even Daddy. It's often the very first word that a Jewish child might say as they learn to talk. And Jesus tells us to call God that name. Nice, huh?

56

Does God have thoughts?

God, your thoughts are precious to me.
They are so many!

Psalm 139:17

Yes! God has all kinds of thoughts, but remember, God is so big we don't always understand what He's thinking. In fact, according to Isaiah 55:8-9, "The Lord says, 'Your thoughts are not like my thoughts. Your ways are not like my ways. Just as the heavens are higher than the earth, so are my ways higher than your ways. And my thoughts are higher than your thoughts.'" Think of it this way: What if you were trying to warn a bunch of ants that an anteater was coming down the street? You might try to shoo them out of the way or tell them to hide, but chances are, they'd just look at you or run away because they were scared. That's kind of how it is with God and us. He's so big and so smart that we don't always understand what He's up to. Aren't you glad He sent Jesus down to us so we could see what God is like?

Here are some other Scriptures that tell us that yes, God has thoughts:

Psalm 139:17: "How precious to me are your thoughts, O God! How vast is the sum of them!" (ESV).

Isaiah 55:9: "For as the heavens are higher than the earth, so are my ways higher than your ways and my thoughts than your thoughts" (ESV).

Jeremiah 29:11: "For I know the plans [thoughts] I have for you, declares the LORD, plans for welfare and not for evil, to give you a future and a hope" (ESV).

You know what God thinks about all day long? Right, YOU!

Why did God make different races?

The Lord said, "Now, these people are united. They all speak the same language. This is only the beginning of what they will do."

Genesis 11:6

According to the Bible (Gen. 1:27), all the people on the earth came from one mom and dad, Adam and Eve. That means there's only one race—humankind! In the *really* early days of history, everybody lived in pretty much one region—not far from the garden of Eden, where Iraq and Iran are now. And God wanted everybody to spread out and populate the earth. But the people didn't like that idea. They wanted to stay in a city called Babel. They even thought they were so cool that they could build a tower that reached heaven. Guess how that turned out?

So God scattered everybody and even confused their language so they started using different words. As they spread out, they became different people groups living all over the region. Especially the Middle East, Africa, and Europe. Notice they were still one race. But different people groups grew, living in different areas and ultimately beginning to look different, depending on where they settled and how they lived.

So the big lesson here is we're all one big family! We're brothers and sisters, and God wants us to love everybody the way He does, no matter what their skin color, the language they speak, or how they look. And He wants us to be thankful that He made all of us different and special.

TALK IT OVER

One Big Family

When God looks at us, He gets excited because He loves us so much. No matter what color we are!

1. According to the Bible, we're all one race because we all came from Adam and Eve. Does that seem confusing to you?

2. Since we're all from the same family and we all have the same Father in heaven, how should we treat people who are different from us?

3. What are some ways people can be different from each other? (Hint: different language, skin color, nationality.)

4. What are some ways we can show God's love this week to someone who's different from us?

Are babies up in heaven just waiting to be born?

You made my whole being.
    You formed me in my mother's body.
I praise you because you made me in an amazing
    and wonderful way.

Psalm 139:13–14

You might hear this sometimes: "Oh, God had a little angel up in heaven with Him, and He sent that child down to earth." That's a really nice thing to say, but truth is, God made each one of us from scratch! Some people think that there are little spirits up in heaven just waiting to be born here on earth. But the Bible says that God creates each one of us from *nothing*. He thought about us, He designed us, and then He put us together inside our moms. He even gave us certain emotions, desires, and talents that He knew before we were born! He knew how tall we were going to be, the color of our hair, and even our favorite food. God knows each and every thing about us and even placed us in the family He had in mind for us since the beginning of the world. Psalm 139:13 says that God formed our inward parts when we were inside our moms! Aren't you glad God made you to be the best *you* you could be?

Is God really watching me all the time?

Only you know what people are really thinking.
1 Kings 8:39

The answer to this question is YES! Somehow God can keep His eye on every single one of us, all at the same time. Remember, God isn't limited by time, so He can be close to all of us at once.

He even knows how many hairs are on your head—before *and* after you get a haircut. God knows your thoughts and the things that make you happy, scared, sad, or mad.

Just think—the God who created all the galaxies also knows and cares about *you*. He even knows your name!

But remember, God's not keeping an eye on you like some grumpy schoolmaster hoping He'll catch you doing something wrong. He's watching you because He wants to be close to you all day and all night. Even while you're asleep. He's as near as your next breath, and He loves and cares for every little thing in your life.

Can we really talk to God?

I call to you, God,
   and you answer me.
Listen to me now.
   Hear what I say.

Psalm 17:6

Absolutely! In fact, you want to know something? God *loves* it when we talk to Him. Talking to God is called praying. And it's a lot easier than you think. Just talk to Him like you would a friend. Tell Him what's going on with you. Tell Him the hard things you're going through and thank Him for all the good things. We'll talk about where and when and how to pray a little bit later in this book, but meanwhile, you can be sure that you can talk to God anytime you want.

Hello? May I speak to God?

If you have something coming up that you need help with, like a test at school, moving to a new place, or even being nice to your brother or sister, tell God about it. Ask for His help. He loves it when we include Him in everything we do.

143

Do we need to use certain words when we pray?

Lord, please teach us how to pray.
Luke 11:1

That's a really good question—in fact, a lot of grown-ups have that same question. But the answer is no. You don't need to talk a certain way or say certain words when you talk to God. Like I said in question 60, God loves it when we talk to Him just like we're talking to a friend. Let's pretend that your family is moving to a new place and you're a little nervous about it. When you're praying, you might say, "Dear Lord, I'm nervous about moving to my new house. Would You help me when I get there?" Let Him know everything you're feeling. "Please help me make friends and get along in school." Something like that.

One thing you do want to remember—God is the Creator of the whole universe, so we always need to remember Who we're talking to. And since He's that big and powerful, He can handle any of our problems and challenges. Nothing is too hard for God!

Luke 1:37 says, "God can do everything," and that's true!

Why does God want us to pray?

Then you will call my name. You will come to me and pray to me. And I will listen to you.

Jeremiah 29:12

God wants us to pray for three reasons:

1. We pray so we can learn to invite Him into everything we do: the good things, the hard things, the funny things, and the challenging things. God's number one priority in the whole world is friendship with us, and praying brings us closer to Him.

2. God knows that a lot of things we face every day might be too big or too hard for us. And if we ask Him to help us, He will, and we'll be successful. Have you ever asked your mom or dad to do something for you that you couldn't do for yourself, like fix something or open something? It's kind of like that. God wants us to ask Him for help.

3. God wants us to learn to do things *with* Him, and praying is a great way to get to know God better. The more we pray, the more we realize that He wants to be involved in everything we do. We can ask for His help, His leading, and even His assistance in making smart decisions. Go ahead. Pray for your mom or dad or aunt or uncle who needs help with something. You can pray for kids or teachers at school, for someone who's sick, or for someone who's having a rough day. When you pray, you're inviting God right into their situation.

Even though I'm a Christian and I love God, I still do bad stuff. What's going on?

I do not understand the things I do. I do not do the good things I want to do. And I do the bad things I hate to do.

Romans 7:15

Whew, this is a *great* question! A lot of people think that when they become a Christian or follower of Jesus, they'll never be tempted to do bad stuff anymore. But unfortunately, that isn't the way it works. We still live in the world, which isn't perfect since Adam and Eve blew it by disobeying God. So, we still have temptations, we get hurt, and sometimes we end up doing something or *saying* something that hurts another person or even ourselves. But the good news is, as you grow in your friendship with Jesus, it's going to become easier to do the right thing, and believe it or not, it'll become harder to do the bad stuff.

By the way, when you do something bad, just tell God you're sorry and ask Him to help you do better in the future.

64

Why do we celebrate Christmas?

Today your Savior was born in David's town. He is Christ, the Lord.

Luke 2:11

Christmas is a wonderful time of the year. Trees, decorations, yummy food, parties, lights, and PRESENTS! But the real reason we celebrate Christmas is because it's the day we remember that God left heaven and came down to earth. Jesus is God in human form,

and He became a baby so He might experience life just the way we all do. And He wasn't born in a palace, surrounded by people waiting on Him and serving Him. He was born in a stable—a cave, actually—surrounded by sheep, cows, and goats. But that was just the way God planned it. He wanted to sneak into our world quietly. And instead of making Jesus's birth known to the kings and leaders of the country, God sent angels to announce it to a bunch of shepherds! So, next December, remember that Christmas is Jesus's birthday.

What are your favorite things about Christmas?

....

....

....

....

....

....

....

....

About December 25

The truth of the matter is nobody really knows exactly when Jesus's birthday actually was. Some people think it must have been in the spring or summer because, in the Luke account, the shepherds were outside taking care of their flocks, something they would normally have done in the warmer weather. People started celebrating Christmas on December 25 around the year AD 354, over three hundred years after Jesus was born, and that has been the traditional date of Christmas ever since.

The important thing is that we celebrate the fact that God visited us in the form of a little baby—the baby Jesus.

65

Why do we call it Good Friday if that was the day Jesus died?

The army officer that was standing there before the cross saw what happened when Jesus died. The officer said, "This man really was the Son of God!"

Mark 15:39

This is a question that's bothered a lot of people throughout history. Jesus spent more than three years going around healing people, doing miracles, and telling everyone He met about God. But that was just one of the reasons He came. The other was to take the punishment for the bad stuff we do. From the time Jesus was born, He never, ever did even one thing wrong! He needed to live a perfect life because none of us could. So, when Jesus was thirty-three years old, the people who hated Him captured Him, held a pretend trial, and took Him to the leader of the Romans in that area, a guy named Pontius Pilate. Even though Pilate didn't find anything wrong that Jesus had done, he still, because of

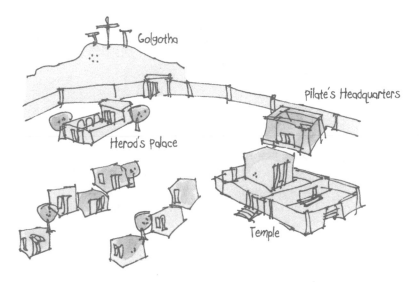

the crowd, sentenced Jesus to death. Death by hanging on a cross.

To Jesus's friends, this looked like a tragic mistake, but it was God's plan all along. That way, Jesus could be the perfect One to take our place, die on the cross, and be separated from the Father. So, even though Good Friday is the day we remember Jesus dying on the cross for us, we call it "good" because Jesus took our bad stuff on Himself and died, one for all, so we would never have to be separated from God again. That's really good!

Good Friday

Good Friday is the day Jesus died. And it was no accident. God had a plan, Jesus followed it, and God's Spirit was involved all the way through.

1. According to this chapter, why is the day Jesus died called Good Friday?

2. Have you ever done anything wrong? Something that hurt you or someone else? Tell about it.

3. Since God is perfect and we couldn't have lived with Him because of the bad stuff we've done, how did Jesus's sacrifice on the cross help us get back to God?

4. Jesus took our place on the cross and was separated from the Father so we never have to be. Because Jesus opened the way, we can live with God forever!

This is a good time to thank God for sending Jesus to take our punishment for the bad stuff we do. Thank God for Good Friday.

Why do we celebrate Easter?

> Why are you looking for a living person here? This is a place for the dead. Jesus is not here. He has risen from death!
>
> Luke 24:5–6

Christmas and Easter are probably the two most important holidays for believers in Jesus. We celebrate Christmas as the birthday of Jesus—the day He came to the world to live as a kid before growing up and showing us what God was like. But Easter is a different kind of celebration. When Jesus was thirty-three years old, His friends deserted Him and He was led off to be crucified. As His friends and followers looked on, Jesus died up there on the cross. It was a dark day. So, a couple of Jesus's followers came and took His body down from the cross, carried Him over to one of their tombs, and buried Him. But the good news is, Jesus didn't stay there. Three days later (Easter Sunday), Jesus was raised from the dead and came back to life! This proved who He was, but it also showed that death had no control over Him. And as a result, it has no control over all of us who follow Jesus! So, even though we might think of flowers, colored eggs, and bunnies on Easter, the real reason we celebrate is because that was the day Jesus rose from the dead.

And, by the way, He's still alive today, so we can be sure that He's with us and He'll always take care of us.

Does God like kids?

Let the little children come to me. Don't stop them.
The kingdom of God belongs to people who are like
these little children.

Mark 10:14

Since Jesus is really God in human form, whenever we look at Him, we can know what God the Father is like. And we know that Jesus loved kids. In fact, in Mark 10, some moms brought their kids to see Jesus. But when the kids showed up, some of Jesus's grown-up friends tried to keep them away. Maybe they thought Jesus was too busy or too important to spend any time with children. Back in Jesus's time, kids weren't taken very seriously, and most of the time they were ignored. But when Jesus's friends tried to keep the kids away, He got mad and told them not to do that. "Let the little children come to me," He said. "Don't stop them." And the kids ran to Jesus and got in His lap, and He blessed them and prayed for them. He might have even rough-housed with them a little bit. Yes, God loves kids!

Draw a picture of you and your friends doing something fun.

Why did Jesus have to die?

The greatest love a person can show is to die for his friends.

John 15:13

Jesus came to earth for two reasons: to show us what God is like and to open up the way for us to get back to the Father. God is a perfect God, pure and holy. But people are, you know, not pure. We do a lot of things that aren't good for us or for the people around us. God calls that sin. Since God is perfect, He can't just ignore the bad stuff we do. It needs to be dealt with. But God loves us so much, He didn't want us to be separated from Him. Someone had to pay the penalty for our bad stuff. So God sent His Son, Jesus, to take the penalty. The religious leaders who hated Jesus held a pretend trial to convict Him. Then they handed Him over to the Roman soldiers, who took Jesus and nailed Him to a cross, which was the way they executed the worst of the prisoners back then. But that wasn't the worst part. While Jesus hung on the cross, He was separated from God the Father for the first time in eternity. Because all of our bad stuff was hung on Jesus, God the Father couldn't be close to Him, so Jesus was left alone on the cross. But the good news is, because of what Jesus did for us, we never have to be separated from God ever. Jesus paid the price.

I still don't understand how Jesus took the penalty for me. How did He do that?

Christ himself died for you. And that one death paid for your sins. He was not guilty, but he died for those who are guilty. He did this to bring you all to God. His body was killed, but he was made alive in the spirit.

1 Peter 3:18

et's use this story as an example: Let's say you break the law by taking someone's car and driving it all over town one night. I know you guys are mostly too young to drive, but go with me here. You drive over people's lawns, the wrong way on a one-way street, through people's living rooms, and into their swimming pools. Finally, the police catch up with you and arrest you. They wake up the judge, and you have to stand before him. As he looks at the list of all your crimes, he says, "You drove into a swimming pool?" and you nod. He takes a long moment and looks through his law book and says,

"For all the crimes you committed tonight, I have to send you to jail for ten years."

"Ten years?" you say.

"I'm afraid so."

So, just as he's about to have you taken to jail, his son walks in.

"What's going on, Dad?" he says. The judge tells his son what happened and the punishment you're about to receive. Then the son looks at you and says, "I don't want you to go away for ten years. Dad, I'd like to take my friend's place." The judge thinks about it and says, "If you're sure, then you can take their place. They'll go free, but you'll have to go to jail." The innocent one takes the punishment for the guilty one.

That's a silly story, but it's pretty much what Jesus did for us. He lived a perfect life and never did anything wrong; then He died and was separated from God in our place. Aren't you glad He did that?

I still don't understand how Jesus took the penalty for me.

Jesus Opened the Door

The bad stuff we do is like a big canyon separating us from God. But Jesus did something that built a bridge to bring us back to God.

1. When Jesus took our place and died on the cross, He opened up the way for us to get back to the Father. Was this a good plan?

2. If Jesus did that for us, what is the one thing we need to do to get back into friendship with God?

3. What's a good thing we can do right now to let God know we're glad He sent Jesus?

If you'd like to start a friendship with God, just follow the ABCs on page 225.

Did Jesus really rise from the dead?

They were saying, "The Lord really has risen from death!"

Luke 24:34

This is a really important question, isn't it? Did Jesus really die on the cross and then come back to life three days later? And is He really alive today? It sounds pretty amazing, doesn't it? And maybe even hard to believe. But we can believe that Jesus died and rose again for several reasons:

1. The disciples told everybody that Jesus had risen from the dead from the very beginning. And most of the disciples even died for their faith as the years went by. If they knew Jesus didn't rise from the dead, surely they would have said so to save their lives!

2. Most of the New Testament was written within a couple decades of Jesus's death. There were people around who would have met and known

Jesus and His disciples. These people would say if their stories weren't true.

3. In Paul's first letter to the Corinthians (1 Cor. 15:6), he says that after Jesus died and rose again, He appeared to His disciples and others and then to over five hundred people at one time! Paul goes on to say that most of those people were still alive when he wrote the letter.

By the way, all the leaders of the other world religions died and were buried. You can visit most of their graves today. Jesus's tomb is the only one that's empty. That's because He's not there. He's alive!

An Interesting Roman Law

In 1878, an ancient Roman stone slab was dug up that said it was illegal to remove a body from a stone-sealed tomb. Scientists dated the slab back to AD 41, which was about seven years after Jesus was crucified. Apparently, moving a body was such a serious offense that the punishment for it was death. After Jesus died, was buried (in a stone-sealed tomb!), and rose again, a rumor was started that His disciples came at night and stole His body. Could that be why the Romans issued this new law?

What's heaven like?

[God] will wipe away every tear from their eyes. There will be no more death, sadness, crying, or pain. All the old ways are gone.

Revelation 21:4

There are a few descriptions of heaven in the Bible, but even they seem kind of vague and unclear. The Bible talks about streets of gold and huge, beautiful gates. A lot of people—maybe even you—think about heaven as though it's clouds and angels and people sitting around playing harps. But it's not going to be like that at all. In his book *The Last Battle*, a really great writer named C. S. Lewis described heaven the best. He predicted that heaven will be more real, more solid, than anything we've ever known on earth. The colors will be brighter, the sounds will be clearer, and the smells will be, well . . . heavenly. Think of the coolest place you've ever been. Maybe a lake or the ocean or a beautiful mountain you've visited. Well, heaven is a million times better than that. And the best part is that Jesus is there. One thing the Bible promises is that, in heaven, there will be no more hurt, sickness, sadness, or death. And if you've begun a friendship with Jesus, you'll live there forever. Pretty cool, huh?

Draw a picture of what you think heaven looks like.

Is there a McDonald's in heaven?

> Then the king sent other servants. He said to them, "Tell those who have been invited that my feast is ready."
>
> Matthew 22:4

Wow, good thinking. I mean, what's better than McDonald's? And could it be that there might just be one of these fast-food, fun places in heaven? Well, probably not. Like I mentioned before, heaven is going to be amazing! Bigger and brighter and more colorful and real than anything we've ever known. And we won't have to worry about buying food or groceries. Jesus sometimes talked about God's big banquet. And guess what? You're invited, and it's not a potluck! You don't have to bring (or buy) anything! Our perfect heavenly Father will supply all the food and drinks we want.

And believe it or not, they'll be better than a Big Mac or Chicken McNuggets. Talk about a Happy Meal!

Make a list of or draw your five favorite foods.

....

....

....

....

....

73

Is there really a hell? What's it like?

Those people will be punished. . . . They will not be allowed to be with the Lord, and they will be kept away from his great power.

2 Thessalonians 1:9

Yeah, there is an actual place called hell. Jesus talked about it a lot. But hell wasn't created for people. Hell was originally created for the devil and his followers, the demons. Way back before the world was created, the devil (whose name was Lucifer) served God and even led the angels in worship. But when he got proud, he rebelled against God and even tried to *be* God. So God cast Lucifer and the angels who followed him out of heaven.

So now the devil looks for ways to rip off God's people. And sometime in the future, God will send the devil and the angels who followed him to hell where they'll stay forever.

God doesn't want anybody to go to hell. Jesus described it as a place of punishment, darkness, and even fire. But the worst part is, hell is completely cut off and separated from God. All of His goodness (like trees, animals, beauty, flowers, music, and other people) is gone. You're away from your friends and family and totally alone.

But the good news is nobody EVER has to go to hell! Jesus made it possible for us to live in heaven with Him forever.

By the way, even though the devil is really strong, he's not anything like God. He can't be everywhere at once, he doesn't know what's going to happen in the future, and he can't read your mind. It's good to be aware that the devil wants to trip you up, but the most important thing is to always keep your eyes on Jesus.

Why would God send someone to hell?

He who believes in God's Son is not judged guilty.

John 3:18

Like we talked about in the last question, it's never been God's desire that people should go to hell. In fact, God did the most amazing thing to keep all of us from ever going to hell. He sent His own Son, Jesus, to die on the cross and take our punishment for all our sin (all the bad stuff we do, think, or say, remember?). Since Jesus lived a perfect life, He was the only One who could take our place—the innocent for the guilty—and die for our sins. So God did everything He could so that we'll never have to experience hell. Our part is to believe that God did that, to thank Him, and to start following Jesus.

75

Do I have to be good to go to heaven?

They said to him, "Believe in the Lord Jesus and you will be saved."

Acts 16:31

A lot of people think that if you're good enough, you can go to heaven and have a friendship with God and Jesus. But how good do you have to be? Have you ever done anything or said anything that hurt yourself or another person? If you have, then you've sinned. Wow, really? There's only one person in the whole history of the universe who never did anything wrong. He never even had a bad thought! And that's Jesus. That's why He was the perfect One to take our place and receive the punishment for all the bad stuff we've done. So, the answer is no, you can never be good enough to get to heaven. Jesus already took care of that. He opened up the way to heaven for us if we just believe in Him. But God still wants us to be good and obedient and to do good things for people around us. And as we begin to follow Jesus, that becomes easier. God is happy to help you do that when you ask Him to.

DID YOU KNOW?

In the Old Testament book of Genesis, we meet a young guy named Joseph. He was his dad's favorite son (out of twelve!) and got all sorts of extra privileges. And guess what? Joseph's brothers didn't like him very much. His dad even made Joseph what the Bible describes as "a tunic of many colors" (Gen. 37:3 NKJV). It was the kind of coat a prince would wear. Another description of the coat is that it was long-sleeved. In those days, people who worked really hard in the field or tended animals wore short-sleeved coats or coats with no sleeves at all. So, if you wore a long-sleeved coat, you probably didn't have to work very hard. Are you beginning to see why Joseph's brothers hated him and were jealous of him?

Are you your parents' favorite child? Don't tell your brothers and sisters.

76

Will I look the same in heaven? Will my family and friends recognize me?

The follower whom Jesus loved said to Peter, "It is the Lord!"

John 21:7

Lots of people have lots of ideas about this question. Let's look for the answers in God's Word, the Bible:

1. **Jesus appears to His disciples (Luke 24:36–43).** Even though the new bodies that God will give us in heaven will live forever and not be affected by sickness, injury, or death, it seems like we'll look somewhat the same as we do now. After all, when Jesus was raised from the dead and appeared to His disciples, they all recognized Him. He had His new, forever body, but they still knew who He was. (Luke 24:13–16 mentions a couple guys who didn't recognize Jesus after He rose, but it seems that Jesus did that on purpose.)

2. **Jesus's body is real, not a spirit (John 20:24–29).**
   We'll have real, solid bodies in heaven. We won't
   be like spirits or ghosts moving around, but we'll
   be as real as we are now—actually, more real.
   After He rose from the dead, Jesus told His disciple Thomas to touch His body where He'd been
   nailed to the cross and stabbed by a spear. So
   Jesus had a real, solid body, and apparently we
   will too.

Cool Things Jesus Could Do after His Resurrection

He could vanish and go somewhere else. (Luke 24:31)
He could eat. (Luke 24:41–42)
He could move through locked doors. (John 20:19)

77

Will there be cars in heaven?

Then a chariot and horses of fire appeared. The chariot and horses of fire separated Elijah from Elisha. Then Elijah went up to heaven in a whirlwind.

2 Kings 2:11

Wow, good question! Everything we can find about heaven says that it's perfect, there will be no more sickness or pain or death, and everyone will be really close to God. It's outside of everything we know about time and space, and it'll be so much better than we can even imagine. But as far as cars go, it doesn't appear that we'll need them. After all, Jesus seemed to be able to get around pretty easily after He was raised from the dead. He appeared in the room with the disciples (and the doors were locked!), and He disappeared after having a meal with a couple other friends. Also check out the story of Philip in Acts 8:26–40. He told this guy from Ethiopia about Jesus; then the passage says that the Spirit of the Lord took Philip away, and he ended up in Azotus, more than eighteen miles away. And in 2 Kings, Elijah went to heaven in a whirlwind (and maybe a chariot of fire!), so it doesn't look like we'll need cars to get around in heaven. And the best news is—there won't be any traffic jams either!

78

I know somebody who swears a lot and uses bad language. Does that mean they'll go to hell when they die?

When you talk, you should always be kind and wise. Then you will be able to answer everyone in the way you should.

Colossians 4:6

God really does want us to use our words wisely, and He takes our speech very seriously, but how we talk doesn't determine if we're going to miss out on heaven and be separated from God forever. As we talked about in questions 68 and 69, we all fall short of God's perfect standard, so the only way we can be saved from the bad stuff we do is to thank God for sending Jesus to take our punishment and to start a friendship with Him. But as a follower of Jesus, it's really important that we talk in a way that makes Him shine!

79

What about people who have never heard of Jesus? What happens to them?

> But since the beginning of the world those things have been easy to understand. They are made clear by what God has made.
>
> Romans 1:20

This is a question that has bothered people for thousands of years. And there are a few things we need to remember when we think about what happens to people who have never heard of Jesus:

1. God is always fair, just, and kind. Even though we don't have all the answers to all the questions we ask, we can always know that God will do everything perfectly. He knows what's in each and every one of our hearts. So we can trust that He'll always do the right thing.

2. God reveals Himself to people in lots of ways, like in the beauty and wonder of nature. The Bible

also says that He's put something inside each one of us, a little voice or thought that tells us there's something a lot bigger out there, someone who's created everything and knows us like a friend (we know it's God). Check out Romans 1:19–20: "Yes, God has clearly shown them everything that may be known about him. There are things about God that people cannot see—his eternal power and all the things that make him God. But since the beginning of the world those things have been easy to understand. They are made clear by what God has made."

3. It's not up to us to decide who goes to heaven and who doesn't. Our most important job is to love God and let people know how much He loves them. God wants us to share the good things He's done for us with other people so they can get to know Him too.

By the way, this is a really good question that we can trust God with. Meanwhile, we need to get to know God for ourselves and follow Him the best we can.

TALK IT OVER

Sharing God's Best Gift

God's gift of having life forever with Him is the best gift ever. It can be fun to share gifts we're given with others, and we should tell our friends about the best gift we've ever been given . . . eternal life with God!

1. Since God wants everyone to know Him and live together with Him in heaven, what are some ways we can help others get to know Him?

2. What's the first thing we can do when we want a friend to know about Jesus? (Hint: Pray for them.)

3. How can we show God's love to people who don't know Him?

4. Who first told you about Jesus? How did they do that?

Is there someone you can think of who needs to be introduced to Jesus? Take a few minutes to pray that God will show up in that person's life.

80

I watched my friend get baptized at church. What does that mean?

Peter said to them, "Change your hearts and lives and be baptized, each one of you, in the name of Jesus Christ for the forgiveness of your sins."

Acts 2:38

Baptism is a sign that you're a new person now that you've started following Jesus. In a lot of churches, people get baptized by a pastor pouring a little water on the top of their head. In other churches, the person being baptized steps down into a tank of water. Then a pastor leans them back into the water and lifts them out again. (Don't worry, they bring them up really quickly.) If you don't know what this is all about, you might think it's a little strange. But here's what it means: When the pastor lowers you into the water, it's like your old self is being buried. Then when they bring you up out of the water again, it's like you're a new person!

Jesus told His followers to get baptized, so that's a good reason to do it. It's a good thing for you to do because you can always remember the day you were baptized, and it helps you remember that Jesus is making you a new person. Also, it's good for your friends and family to watch you get baptized because it shows them that now you're following Jesus.

Does it matter how I speak to people?

What you say can mean life or death.
Those who love to talk will be rewarded for what
they say.

Proverbs 18:21

God really does care about how we talk to one another. If you've ever been hurt by someone calling you a name or saying that you were stupid, then you know how bad that feels. Since we're God's kids, He doesn't like it when we're hurting. And He doesn't want us to hurt anyone else. Proverbs 18:21 says, "What you say can mean life or death." This means we can either hurt people with our words or make them feel good. So, if you want to make God smile, you need to speak kindly to everyone you meet (even your little brother!). We should always build each other up, not tear each other down. Let's decide to speak life to one another!

185

Do I really have to love people I don't like? How can I do that?

But I tell you, love your enemies. Pray for those who hurt you.

Matthew 5:44

Jesus says He wants us to treat people, friends and enemies alike, the way we'd like to be treated. Do you like to be bullied, made fun of, or hurt? Didn't think so. Jesus knows that kind of behavior isn't good for anybody. It hurts the person being made fun of, and it hurts the one who's doing it. He wants us to love other people. But He also knows it's hard to love some of the people in our lives. So He wants us to ask Him for help. You can pray and say something like this:

Dear Lord, I'm really having a hard time loving _____ [fill in the name here]. Would You please help me to love them and see them the way You do? Thanks a lot. Amen.

Praying for a difficult person will help soften your heart toward them, so try praying for them.

By the way, if somebody is hurting you, bullying you, or doing something to you that you know is wrong, you need to tell somebody about it. God doesn't want you to go through stuff like that.

Why doesn't God just make us all follow Him?

> I am offering you life or death, blessings or curses. Now, choose life!
>
> Deuteronomy 30:19

God loves us too much to make us follow Him like a bunch of robots. God could have programmed all of us to follow Him and do whatever He said all the time. But He didn't do that. At the very beginning of time, God gave Adam and Eve (and all people) the choice to follow Him or not. And remember how that turned out?

Imagine if someone was forced to be your friend. They didn't really want to, but they had to because their parents made them. Their friendship wouldn't mean much

to you, would it? Well, God didn't want that to happen, so He gave us the free choice to be His friend or not. That's why it means so much to Him when we choose to follow Him, talk to Him, and tell others about Him. God doesn't want us to be robots!

TALK IT OVER

Free to Choose

Even though God could have made all of us believe in Him and follow Him, He left the choice up to us. He didn't want robots; He wanted close friendships.

1. According to the Bible, God gave Adam and Eve the choice to obey Him or not. What happened when they chose to disobey and eat the fruit?

2. Share about a time when you disobeyed or made a bad choice. What happened?

3. Would you like it if a friend was forced to hang out with you even if they didn't like you?

4. What would happen if God made all of us obey Him even if we didn't want to?

Pray for God to give you wisdom to make right choices.

Does God want me to be kind to animals?

A good man takes care of his animals.

Proverbs 12:10

Everything on earth—people, animals, trees, plants, and fish—was all created by God. And the cool thing is, when God created Adam and Eve, He gave them the job of taking care of and tending all of it. And even though lots has changed since those early days in the garden of Eden, some things haven't changed. One of those things is our duty to take care of animals. Some people do that for a job, like ranchers, zookeepers, and trainers, but if you have a dog, cat, rabbit, or gerbil, God wants *you* to take good care of them too. God gives us the task of making sure they're fed and taken care of. In fact, some of the people in the Bible were full-time animal keepers. King David started out caring for sheep. So did Moses. And guess who were the first people the angels appeared to when Jesus was born? A group of shepherds, that's who. So, evidently God thinks it's important to take care of animals.

Lots of times, animals can't completely take care of themselves, whether it's an injured bird, a porpoise who's caught in a net, or a stray kitten. And guess who gets to help them? That's right—you and me!

Is it important for me to take care of the earth?

The Lord God put the man in the garden of Eden to care for it and work it.

Genesis 2:15

Since God created the world and it belongs to Him (check out Ps. 24:1), we can honor God by honoring His creation. Sometimes people do things that hurt the earth, like dumping garbage and chemicals into rivers and oceans or killing animals to the point of wiping them out altogether. But this is not how we honor God. When He created Adam, God told Him to take care of the garden, which was pretty much the entire world at that point. And God wants *us* to take good care of His creation too. God made us in His image and to be higher and smarter than the animals, and He also gave us the responsibility to take care of the earth.

What are some ways you can help take care of the earth? (Hint: Don't throw trash around. Recycle things if you can. Don't waste food.)

How does God help people nowadays?

I was in trouble. So I called to the Lord.
The Lord answered me and set me free.

Psalm 118:5

In Bible times, God would sometimes do some really big miracles to help His people. Like when He opened up the Red Sea so they could walk through and escape from Pharaoh's army (Exod. 14). At other times, God would send hail or floods to defeat an enemy army, and once He even made the sun stand still to help Israel in a battle (Josh. 10:12–15)!

But does He still do big, miraculous things today? Yes, He does!

God still helps people in these ways:

1. God *still* does big miracles today. He still heals people from diseases, miraculously supplies food and other things to people in need, and sometimes even controls the weather in order to help people.

2. God also helps people today through us! Have you ever seen how God's people respond when there's a natural disaster, like a flood, tornado, or hurricane? Lots of churches and Christian groups get together and help the victims of those disasters. God wants His people to be His hands and feet and help the poor, the lost, and even the people in our own neighborhoods, schools, and families.

3. And lots of times, things work out really well and people don't realize that God is behind it. They think there are just a lot of coincidences that happen, but we know that God's really working something out. When those things happen, be on the lookout for what God is up to.

Can you think of some ways you might help somebody you know?

....

....

....

....

Why are we supposed to worship God?

Come into his city with songs of thanksgiving.
  Come into his courtyards with songs of praise.
  Thank him, and praise his name.

Psalm 100:4

There are lots of reasons to worship God and lots of ways to do it. Let's look at one of the reasons why we should worship God: He's totally worth it! I mean, He's the Creator of the whole universe, and He's also powerful enough to know every single one of us. Think of it this way: If a royal king or queen were to show up at your house, how would you react? You'd honor and welcome them, give them your best chair to sit in, and make a really yummy dinner for them. Why? Because they're the king or the queen! Well, if you remember that God is the King of everything, then it's totally good and right to let Him know how much you love and appreciate Him.

What are some ways you can worship God? Well, if you're in a group at church, Sunday school, or camp, you might sing songs to Him. You can worship Him by being grateful and telling Him what you're thankful for. Another way you can worship Him is by reminding yourself how great and awesome He is. In other words, you can worship God anywhere and anytime.

Why are there so many different churches?

A person's body is one thing, but it has many parts. Yes, there are many parts to a body, but all those parts make only one body. Christ is like that too.

1 Corinthians 12:12

God started the first church forty days after Jesus went up to heaven. The first leader was Jesus's good friend Peter. He told people about Jesus and God's plan for bringing us back into friendship with Him, and over three thousand people responded that day by following Jesus!

One of the leaders of that early church was Jesus's brother James. As history continued, people had different ideas of what should be important in their gatherings. And even though they all believed in Jesus, they didn't always agree with each other on some things. Some people liked the service to be in a different language, some liked it to be informal, others liked it to be more formal, and some liked a lot of music in their services. So different church groups sprang up. Now there are thousands of groups or denominations around the world. And people can find a church that fits with what they believe as well as how they feel comfortable worshiping. God doesn't mind the different denominations as long as they all worship Jesus, believe His Word, and love and care for one another.

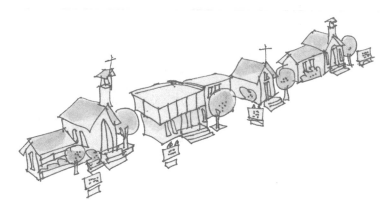

TALK IT OVER

Lots of People, Lots of Churches

There are many denominations around the world today worshiping God and growing in His Word. People worship God with different kinds of music and services and even in different languages!

1. With over 2.3 billion followers of Jesus in the world, what are the chances that people with all those different cultures, personalities, likes, and dislikes would want to go to the same church?

2. Name some things you really like about the church you attend. If you don't go to a church right now, what are some things you'd like in a church? (Hint: good music, an interesting pastor with good stories, fun kid activities, etc.)

3. Even though lots of people go to lots of different churches, what are the three most important things to look for in a church? (Hint: love for Jesus, belief in God's Word, and love for other people.)

4. If you were in charge of a church, what things would you include? Use your imagination and be creative!

Pray for your pastor and the church staff. Or think of a church in your area and pray for them.

Was David a real person or was he make-believe?

> This is what God said about him: "I have found David son of Jesse. He is the kind of man I want. He will do all that I want him to do."
>
> Acts 13:22

For a long time, a lot of people didn't believe David was a real person because, other than in the Bible, nobody ever found any proof that he lived. But then in 1993, archaeologists discovered a carved stone from a country close to Israel that mentioned the king of the House of David. They estimate that the stone goes all the way back to 900 BC. (BC means "before Christ," or before the time that Jesus was here on earth.) So, this stone that mentions David is from just about the time he and his children were ruling Israel. We can read David's story in the books of 1 and 2 Samuel, from his fight with Goliath all the way through David becoming king of the whole nation of Israel. He was a great and mighty king who's mentioned throughout the whole Bible. And now we see that even other kings and countries knew who he was.

Is the story of David and Goliath real?

Everyone gathered here will know the Lord does not need swords or spears to save people. The battle belongs to him!

1 Samuel 17:47

If you've never heard the story of David and Goliath, here's an overview. There was this giant named Goliath who wanted to fight God's people in a place called the Valley of Elah in Israel. And there was a young boy named David who was the only one brave enough to fight the giant. Well, David went to face Goliath with nothing but his sling and a stone. Goliath had armor, a shield, a sword, and a spear. But David surprised the giant by hitting him with a stone shot out of his sling, and David won a great victory that day! Sounds like a made-up fairy tale, doesn't it? Well, here are a few things you need to know:

1. Even though Goliath was really big—even a giant—the Bible says he was about ten feet tall, not fifty feet like the giants in fairy tales.

2. David was probably fifteen or sixteen years old, not a little kid, when he stepped up to fight Goliath.

3. David was an expert with a sling and stone. After all, he'd had a lot of time for target practice as he sat on the hillsides watching his dad's sheep.

So, yes, the story of David and Goliath really happened. You can read the whole thing in 1 Samuel 17.

About David's Sling

David's sling wasn't like the slingshots that are around today. It was a small leather pouch with two long leather straps. A person would put a stone in the pouch and whirl it around over their head. Then they would let go of one of the straps, and the stone would sail out at around sixty miles an hour.

Draw a picture of David and Goliath.

91

Why did Jesus pray?

I pray for these men. But I am also praying for all people who will believe in me because of the teaching of these men.

John 17:20

If Jesus is God, why did He have to pray? That's a really good question and one that can be confusing. Now, remember Jesus is God's *Son*, so when He prayed, He was talking to God the *Father*. Here are a few reasons Jesus prayed to His Father:

1. The number one thing in Jesus's life was His relationship with God the Father. While Jesus was here on earth, He was in constant touch with God. He referred to God as *Abba*, a word meaning "Father" or even "Dad." Like how we say "Daddy."

   By the way, back in Jesus's time, nobody called God "Father," much less "Daddy." People thought it was disrespectful to do that. And Jesus even got in trouble a couple times when He called God His

Father. But the great thing is, the Bible tells us to call God "Abba," or "Dad." Check out Romans 8:15.

2. The second reason Jesus prayed was that while He was on earth, He was a person and was limited just like we are. Even though it seems like Jesus could do anything at all, He knew He had to depend on His Father to give Him strength and wisdom for all He needed to do. Not a bad idea for us either. It's always good to ask God for these things.

3. And finally, the third reason Jesus prayed was because He knew that God the Father wanted Him to. And Jesus always wanted to obey God and do what He wanted Him to do.

92

Where do we have to pray?

After sending them away, he went into the hills to pray.

Mark 6:46

When you pray, you should go into your room and close the door.

Matthew 6:6

Some people think you have to be in church to pray to God. Church is a great place to pray, but you can talk to God anytime and anyplace. As you can see in the two verses above, Jesus prayed outside on a mountain, and He told His friends they could pray in their rooms. When you realize that God is everywhere and that He loves it when you talk to Him, then you realize you can pray wherever you are! Let Him know how you're doing today. Ask for His help with school, friends, or family stuff going on. Thank Him for the A you got on a test or the goal you scored in soccer. You can talk to God in the morning, at lunchtime, and right before bed. Remember,

He's your friend and He wants to know all about you and what's going on in your life.

Teach Us to Pray

God loves it when we talk to Him, no matter if we're in church, at school, on the ball field, or in the pool. It doesn't matter where we are, praying is a good thing.

1. Is it hard for you to pray, or is it easy? Explain.

2. Sometimes making a prayer list helps you remember what to pray about. What are some things you'd like to put on that list?

3. Do you ever feel like you have to use certain words when you pray?

4. Jesus taught His disciples to pray using the Lord's Prayer in Matthew 6:9–13. Can you see His pattern for prayer in these verses? (Hint: worship, partnering with His will, asking for our needs to be met, forgiving others, and asking for protection from evil.)

Practice praying in this way with and for one another.

93

Is it okay to be mad when I pray, or should I wait until I'm happy?

People, trust God all the time.
Tell him all your problems.
God is our protection.

Psalm 62:8

It's okay to be sad, mad, or upset when you talk to God. He wants you to be honest with Him, even if things aren't going well at the moment. In fact, when things aren't going well is a great time to pray. Maybe somebody has upset you or you stubbed your toe or you feel lonely or sad. Maybe things are hard at school or with your friends, or maybe you didn't get chosen for the team. These are all good times to pray and let God in on what's going on. You might even ask Him to help you calm down and to help you feel better. Sometimes God allows hard stuff to happen so we'll learn to trust Him and know that He'll help us go through whatever's bothering us.

After you pray, share how you're feeling with an adult you trust. Maybe it's your mom or dad or a teacher, pastor, or coach. God might use them to give you some ideas to help you get through what you're facing.

If you're having trouble praying or just learning how to talk to God, try a practice prayer. You can say something like this:

Dear Lord, I'm kind of upset right now. I feel sad/ mad/lonely/rejected and I need Your help. Help me calm down and feel better. And help me with _____ [fill in the blank with what's bothering you]. Show me if I need to talk to someone about how I'm feeling. Thanks. Amen.

Why do people say "amen" after their prayers?

The "Yes" to all of God's promises is in Christ. And that is why we say "Amen" through Christ to the glory of God.

2 Corinthians 1:20

The word *amen* comes from the original language the Bible was written in—Hebrew. The meaning of *amen* is "truly" or "so be it," so when people say "amen" at the end of their prayers, they're saying, "Please, Lord, hear my prayer and answer my request in the way You see is best." *Amen* is not a magic word or anything, and honestly, after a while people might say it so often they forget what it means. But when you pray and say "amen," remember that you're asking God to hear and answer your prayer.

When is a good time to pray?

Never stop praying.
1 Thessalonians 5:17

You know when is the very best time to pray? Anytime! When you start to think of God as your friend, you can see that, just like a friend at school or in your neighborhood, you can talk to Him whenever you feel like it. Are you sad? Tell God about it and ask Him to help you. Are you happy? Let God know and thank Him for what's making you happy. Some people like to pray first thing in the morning. You can say, *Good morning, Lord. Thanks for a good night's sleep. Help me go with You throughout this day.* A lot of people like to pray right before bed. Just make sure you're not too sleepy or you might doze off in the middle of your prayer! You can say something like *Thanks, Lord, for this great day. Thank You for the new friend I met at school*, or *Thanks for the time I got to play with my sister (or dog) today. Please watch over me as I go to sleep, and see You tomorrow!*

Get the idea?

Why does God take so long to answer our prayers sometimes?

You know that these things are testing your faith. And this will give you patience.

James 1:3

Sometimes when we pray for something, it happens right away. And that's really fun, cool, and exciting. But what about the times when you pray and pray for something, and . . . nothing? Does God not hear? Or are you doing something wrong? Well, there are a couple things to think about in this case:

1. The most important thing to remember is that God always knows what He's doing, and He always knows what's best for us. He might just think it's too early to give you what you prayed for. Maybe you're not ready and He's waiting for you. Maybe He's getting you ready for His best answer yet. A guy in the Bible named Joseph (the

one with the special, cool coat) had to wait over thirteen years for God's answer! Check out his story in Genesis, chapters 37–50.

2. Have you ever eaten an apple before it was fully ripe? Yuck. Well, maybe God's not answering your prayer right now because He's teaching you a bigger lesson as you wait for Him to answer. Maybe, just maybe, God is doing something in you while you wait. He might be teaching you about trusting Him even when you don't see the answer . . . yet.

So, what do you do when God hasn't answered your prayer yet? Keep praying—don't give up! You might also ask God to give you wisdom to know if what you're praying for is really something He wants for you. God wants us to know Him, and sometimes He has something even better for us than what we could ever ask for!

97

Am I really supposed to be good to others? Even my brother?

Then Peter came to Jesus and asked, "Lord, when my brother sins against me, how many times must I forgive him?"

Matthew 18:21

Brothers can be a pain sometimes, can't they? But think of it this way: Maybe they think *you're* a pain sometimes too! So, how are we supposed to treat our brother (or sister for that matter) when they're being annoying? When Jesus was giving a talk that we call "the Sermon on the Mount" (because He was on a mountain at the time), He said, "Do for other people the same things you want them to do for you" (Matt. 7:12). That's pretty simple, isn't it? Jesus wants you to be kind to other people and do stuff for them that you wish they'd do for you. And if you're really having a problem with one of your siblings, sit down with them and your mom or dad and try to figure out a way to deal with it without a major meltdown.

By the way, maybe you should show your brother this book and remind him that God wants him to treat you well too!

98

Why does God want us to be thankful?

Give thanks whatever happens. That is what God wants for you in Christ Jesus.

1 Thessalonians 5:18

God wants us to be thankful because counting the things we're thankful for reminds us of how good God is and all the great things He's done for us. All throughout the Old Testament, God tells His people to *remember*. Remember all the times God kept them safe or helped them in battle, or how He took care of all their needs, like feeding them when there was no food around. By being thankful, we're actually drawing close to God and realizing that He's taken really good care of us all along. And when we know and remember all the great things He's done for us in the past, we can face the future knowing He'll take care of us then too!

When we worry, it's like we're thinking that God won't be there in the future when we need Him. What are the chances of that? (Hint: zero.)

So, even when you're going through hard things, it's good to be thankful—thankful that God cares about you, that He hears you, and that He's going to help you.

Take a couple minutes and write down five things you're thankful for.

....

....

....

....

....

99

Does God want me
to help the poor?

Being kind to the poor is like lending to the Lord.
The Lord will reward you for what you have
done.

Proverbs 19:17

This is an easy one. Yes, He does! Did you know there are millions of people around the world who never have enough to eat? A lot of people don't drink clean water, and some even live in garbage dumps where they have to search for old food just to survive. God has always cared about the poor, and He wants His people—like you—to care about them too.

There are lots of ways to share what you have with people who have less than you:

1. You might consider sponsoring a child in another country through an organization like World Vision, Samaritan's Purse, or Compassion International. It's easy, and even a little money can help them a lot!

2. Support a group in your town that helps the poor and homeless. You might have a rescue mission or church nearby that serves these folks, so ask your parents if you can figure out a way to help them with a donation.

3. You and your family might want to serve at a local mission. You might serve food, help clean up, or just play with some kids who are staying there. Ask someone at your church if your city has a ministry that serves the homeless.

100

When Jesus comes back, is that the end of the world? That sounds scary. When will that happen?

No one knows when that day or time will be. Even the Son and the angels in heaven don't know. Only the Father knows.

Matthew 24:36

God's got this huge plan for us and the world that He came up with even before the beginning of time. And even when things seem crazy around us, we can always be sure that God's still in control. Part of His plan is for Jesus to come back; only this time, instead of a quiet entry like He had that first Christmas in Bethlehem, Jesus is going to come back as the King and Ruler of everything! But in some ways, this isn't the end— it's really only the beginning. God has a perfect world planned, where there will be no more hurt, fear, pain, or death. So, if you're a friend of Jesus now, you have nothing to fear when He comes back. It'll be the beginning of a wonderful forever life with Jesus.

Nobody knows exactly when Jesus is going to come back to rule the world. Even He didn't know while He was here on earth as a human. Only God the Father knows when Jesus will return. But it'll be in God's perfect timing. So, what do you do till then? The best thing to do is get to know Jesus a little more each day, obey Him, and look for chances to serve other people. If you do those things, you'll be more than ready when Jesus returns!

101

Does God like pizza?

So if you eat, or if you drink, or if you do anything, do everything for the glory of God.

1 Corinthians 10:31

You would think so. I mean, who doesn't like pizza? A yummy crust, layers of gooey cheese, and can we talk about the toppings? Pepperoni, chicken, pineapple, tomatoes, salami, olives, and bacon! Makes you hungry just thinking about it. But since God isn't a person, He doesn't need to eat or drink anything, so He's probably never actually tasted pizza. But since He loves us and wants us to enjoy everything He's given us, I'd say He *loves* pizza. Because it makes us happy. He'd probably also say He wouldn't want us to eat a diet of nothing but pizza because He knows we need fruits, vegetables, and other things that make us grow up happy and healthy. But every so often, I think God loves when we eat something we really like (even if it isn't pizza). And it's even better when we're eating and enjoying it with good friends.

You might even say, "Blessed are the pizza makers!" Or maybe not.

How do I become a Christian?

Becoming a Christian is simply deciding to follow Jesus, getting to know Him, and becoming best friends with Him. Even though it seems a little hard sometimes—mainly because you can't *see* Jesus—beginning a friendship with Him is as easy as ABC.

Admit that you do bad stuff and that there's no way you can ever be good enough to go to heaven.

Believe that Jesus is who He said He is—God's Son, who lived a perfect life and then went to the cross, died, and was separated from the Father so we never have to be. Also believe that Jesus beat death by rising from the dead to live forever.

Confess that Jesus isn't just your best friend but the King, the Ruler, the Boss of your life, and follow Him wherever He leads you.

Daily Reading Plan

Here's a simple, easy Bible reading plan for you to try. It goes for thirty days and covers the first seven chapters of the book of Luke (even though a few verses aren't included). Try reading for five minutes a day. If you miss one, not to worry! Just pick up the next day where you left off. At the end of thirty days, keep on going!

☐ **DAY 1: Read Luke 1:1–12**
Zechariah Meets an Angel

☐ **DAY 2: Read Luke 1:13–20**
The Angel's Message

☐ **DAY 3: Read Luke 1:21–25**
Zechariah's Happy News

☐ **DAY 4: Read Luke 1:26–38**
An Angel Visits Mary

☐ **DAY 5: Read Luke 1:39–56**
Mary Goes to See Elizabeth

☐ **DAY 6: Read Luke 2:1–20**
Jesus Is Born!

☐ **DAY 7: Read Luke 2:21–35**
Mary, Joseph, and Jesus

☐ **DAY 8: Read Luke 2:39–50**
Twelve-Year-Old Jesus Gets Left Behind in Jerusalem

☐ **DAY 9: Read Luke 2:51–52**
Jesus Grows Up

☐ **DAY 10: Read Luke 3:1–6**
John the Baptist

☐ **DAY 11: Read Luke 3:7–22**
John the Baptist and Jesus

☐ **DAY 12: Read Luke 4:1–13**
Jesus Is Tempted

☐ **DAY 13: Read Luke 4:14–27**
Jesus Goes to His Hometown

☐ **DAY 14: Read Luke 4:31–37**
Jesus Casts Out an Evil Spirit

☐ **DAY 15: Read Luke 4:38–44**
Jesus Heals a Lot of People

☐ **DAY 16: Read Luke 5:1–11**
Jesus Goes Fishing

☐ **DAY 17: Read Luke 5:12–16**
Jesus Heals a Man with Leprosy

☐ **DAY 18: Read Luke 5:17–26**
Through the Roof!

☐ **DAY 19: Read Luke 5:27–39**
Levi the Tax Collector

☐ **DAY 20: Read Luke 6:1–11**
Jesus Heals on the Sabbath

☐ **DAY 21: Read Luke 6:12–19**
More Disciples, More Healing

☐ **DAY 22: Read Luke 6:20–26**
Jesus's Good Advice

☐ **DAY 23: Read Luke 6:27–36**
Love Your Enemies

☐ **DAY 24: Read Luke 6:37–42**
Forgive Others

☐ **DAY 25: Read Luke 6:43–49**
Build Your Life on the Rock

☐ **DAY 26: Read Luke 7:1–10**
Jesus and the Roman Soldier

☐ **DAY 27: Read Luke 7:11–17**
Jesus Gives a Boy New Life

☐ **DAY 28: Read Luke 7:18–23**
John the Baptist's Question for Jesus

☐ **DAY 29: Read Luke 7:24–35**
Jesus Describes John the Baptist

☐ **DAY 30: Read Luke 7:36–50**
A Thankful Woman

Sandy Silverthorne has been writing and illustrating books since 1988, with nearly one million copies sold. He is the award-winning creator of the Great Bible Adventure children's series, *Crack Yourself Up Jokes for Kids*, *Made You Laugh!*, and *The Best Worst Dad Jokes*. Sandy has worked as a cartoonist, author, illustrator, actor, pastor, speaker, and comedian. Apparently, it's hard for him to focus. Connect with him at www.sandysilverthorne books.com.

Need some laughs?
Check out Sandy's jokes for kids!

When does a joke become a dad joke?
When it's fully groan.

Filled with more than five hundred groan-worthy jokes to torment your kids, this collection makes it possible for you to fill any moment of dead air with a joke that will have everyone within hearing distance rolling their eyes and edging away to avoid association with you.

Learn More about
SANDY

Head to **sandysilverthornebooks.com**
for jokes, Bible stories and lessons,
drawing tutorials, and more!